THE INDOMITABLE
MARY EASTON SIBLEY

Project Sponsors

Western Historical Manuscript Collection–Columbia

Special Thanks
Christine Montgomery
Sara Przybylski
    State Historical Society of Missouri, Columbia

MISSOURI HERITAGE READERS
General Editor, Rebecca B. Schroeder

Each Missouri Heritage Reader explores a particular aspect of the state's rich cultural heritage. Focusing on people, places, historical events, and the details of daily life, these books illustrate the ways in which people from all parts of the world contributed to the development of the state and the region. The books incorporate documentary and oral history, folklore, and informal literature in a way that makes these resources accessible to all Missourians.

Intended primarily for adult new readers, these books will also be invaluable to readers of all ages interested in the cultural and social history of Missouri.

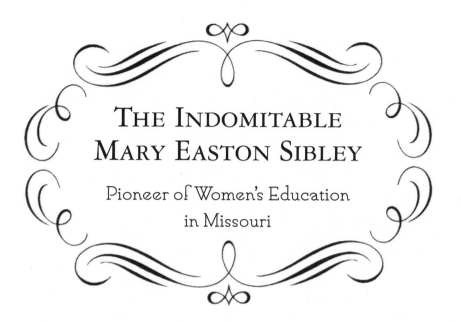

THE INDOMITABLE
MARY EASTON SIBLEY

Pioneer of Women's Education
in Missouri

KRISTIE C. WOLFERMAN

University of Missouri Press
Columbia and London

Library of Congress Cataloging-in-Publication Data

Wolferman, Kristie C., 1948–
  The indomitable Mary Easton Sibley : pioneer of women's education in Missouri /
Kristie C. Wolferman.
    p. cm.
  Includes bibliographical references and index.
  Summary: "Drawing on Mary and George Sibley's journals and letters, Wolferman
brings to life one of Missouri's most remarkable women educators, the founder of
Lindenwood University. Sibley's views regarding women's social and political roles, slav-
ery, temperance, religion, and other topics reflect educational and social developments on
the frontier and nationwide"—Provided by publisher.
  ISBN 978-0-8262-1805-6 (alk. paper)
  1. Sibley, Mary Easton, 1800–1878. 2. Women educators—Missouri—Biography.
3. Women—Education—Missouri—History—19th century. I. Title.
  LA2317.S584W65 2008
  370.92—dc22
  [B]
                                                                        2008015672

♾™ This paper meets the requirements of the
American National Standard for Permanence of Paper
for Printed Library Materials, Z39.48, 1984.

Designer: Stephanie Foley
Typesetter: FoleyDesign
Printer and binder: Thomson-Shore, Inc
Typefaces: Garamond and Minion

The University of Missouri Press gratefully acknowledges the support of anonymous
donors who believe in and wish to sustain the Missouri Heritage Readers Series

Contents

PREFACE

Mary Smith Easton Sibley had beauty, determination, social promi-
nence, and intelligence. All are valuable qualities for a woman of any
generation, but they were especially valuable during the early nineteenth century when men were considered, in Mrs. Sibley's own words
in her journal, to be "the nobler sex . . . superior in knowledge, as they
are in strength and energy of character." Mary Sibley also knew how
to use her attributes to accomplish her own goals, and she left a last-
ing legacy in Lindenwood University in St. Charles, Missouri.

When she was interviewed in 1919 for the *Lindenwood Bulletin*,
Louise Gibson Conn, Mary Sibley's great-niece, remembered her
aunt as "always a very original, dominant character . . . what she
wanted, she got. She went after it and got it, irrespective of everything else." What Mary Sibley "got" was a boarding-school education
in Kentucky, a husband who promoted her interests, classes for
Indian and immigrant children at Fort Osage, an African school and
a Presbyterian church for St. Charles, and the first college for women
west of the Mississippi. Although in her journal Mary lamented her
tendencies toward procrastination and indolence, few nineteenth-
century women accomplished as much. Not only did Mary Sibley
start Lindenwood College, which today is a thriving and expanding
university of approximately fourteen thousand students, but she
also worked for educational opportunities for women and minority
groups including African Americans, Native Americans, and
immigrants.

Mary Sibley's religious awakening in 1832 led her to attack her
causes with missionary zeal. Joining the church also inspired Mary to
keep a record of her religious investigations, testimonies of her faith,

and justifications for her actions. On March 29, 1832, the day Mary applied for admission to the Presbyterian Church, she began her journal, intending, she wrote, "to put down here an account of my opinions and feelings as I progress in my Christian career." Mary kept her journal fairly regularly during 1832, recorded her thoughts more sporadically in 1833, and then made scattered entries up until 1858. Justifying her ideas on religious grounds, both inside and outside her journal, Mary Sibley expressed attitudes that were far ahead of her time. As Mary proselytized, she practiced what she preached on temperance, suffrage for women, and education for women and underprivileged minorities. Although social and political conditions for women and African Americans did not improve much during Mary's lifetime, she was not afraid to express her opinions on changes she thought should occur.

Being an educator was a lifelong role for Mary Sibley. As the eldest child in a family of eleven, she was expected to help teach her younger siblings. Devoted to her father, a prominent attorney who held several official posts in early St. Louis, she learned much from him, from her mother, and from her boarding-school experience. After she married George Sibley and moved with him to Fort Osage where he served as a factor, she began to help Indian children learn how to read and write. When the fort was closed and the Sibleys moved to St. Charles, Mary's role as educator resumed. She took girls into her home to teach and later established Lindenwood, while at the same time teaching immigrant and slave children at a Sunday school. Always the educator, she was also well qualified to assume the role of hostess to a variety of prominent guests, first in her parents' home, then at Fort Osage, and later in St. Charles. Only someone with great energy, and with no tendencies toward either indolence or procrastination, could have accomplished so much.

Acknowledgments

My thanks go to librarian Suzanne Jackson and archivist Paul Huffman at Lindenwood University for allowing me access to Mary Sibley's journal and her other personal papers and books. I also appreciate the help of Bill Popp, archivist of St. Charles County Historical Society, of David Boutros at the Western Historical Manuscript Collection–Kansas City, and of the research assistance provided by the staff of the Missouri Historical Society in St. Louis, the University of Missouri–Kansas City library, and the Sandhills Community College.

I want to acknowledge Lindsy Myers and Mitchell Douglass, who did some "fieldwork" for me in Lexington, Kentucky. I also want to thank my best friends and my family, who put up with my endless ruminations on Mary Sibley.

Special thanks, however, are due to my tireless, relentless editor, Rebecca B. Schroeder; to Jane Lago, managing editor of the University of Missouri Press, for her valuable guidance; and to my husband for making many research trips and for reading and rereading chapters until they were "right."

I am also grateful to the institutions and individuals that gave me permission to reproduce the illustrations included herein, as credited in the text of the book.

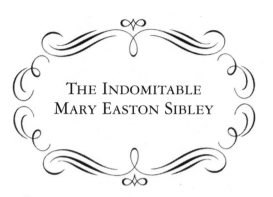

The Indomitable
Mary Easton Sibley

CHAPTER I

The Eastons Arrive in St. Louis

Mary Easton Sibley was born in Rome, New York, on January 24, 1800, the first child of Rufus and Alby Abial Easton. Her father was born to a Connecticut family that had emigrated from England in the 1640s and helped found Hartford. After he completed the schooling available in Litchfield, Rufus Easton studied in a well-known law school conducted by Ephraim Kirby and was admitted to the bar in New York. He started his career in Rome, New York, where he met and married fifteen-year-old Alby Abial Smith in 1798. Abial, like her husband, was descended from an educated colonial family.

Described by historian Charles van Ravenswaay as "ambitious and restless," Easton hoped to use the political and social connections he had developed in New York to gain an appointment as a federal judge. In 1802 he tried unsuccessfully for a judgeship in New York. Through his friend Postmaster General Gideon Granger, he learned of a postmaster position in Ithaca, New York, but in a letter of April 23, 1802, Granger reported that to his regret he could not get Easton the Ithaca position, as it had been committed.

In 1803, as rumors spread of U.S. efforts to purchase New Orleans, Easton thought the West might provide the kind of position he wanted. Hoping for an appointment in the District of New Orleans, he decided to go to Washington, D.C., and apply personally to the president. Dewitt Clinton, a prominent member of the New York Republican Party, advised him to arm himself with "respectable rec-ommendations." Easton solicited a recommendation from Vice President Aaron Burr, which he included in an introductory letter to the president on December 27, 1803.

Apparently Easton did not realize that President Jefferson did not look kindly on recommendations for positions from the man who had jeopardized his election in 1800 by tying the electoral vote, and he was becoming increasingly suspicious of his vice president's ambition and weary of the flood of job requests that Burr passed to him. In addition to Burr, Gideon Granger put in a good word for Easton, but nothing came of either the recommendations or Easton's trip to the capital city.

Even without the promise of a job, Easton decided to move to New Orleans, practice law there, and wait for a government position to open. In the summer of 1804 he began the journey west with his wife and their three children. Mary was four; Joanna Alby Easton was three; and the baby, Louisa, was only a few months old. Again armed with a letter from Aaron Burr, written on March 11, 1804, shortly after the Louisiana Purchase had been announced, Easton thought there might be a possibility of a judgeship or postmaster position in Upper Louisiana, the designation the Spanish colonial government had given the northern part of the Louisiana Territory. To inquire about possible opportunities, he had again written to his friend Gideon Granger. In a letter dated July 7, 1804, Granger discouraged the idea, informing Easton that all the officers for Upper Louisiana had been selected and "There is nothing extra."

During a stopover in Vincennes, the capital of Indiana Territory, Easton happened on the elusive opportunity he had been seeking. When he met with territorial governor William Henry Harrison to present his substantial credentials and inquire about possible positions, he learned of the untimely death of Ephraim Kirby, his former law professor. President Jefferson had appointed Kirby attorney general of the District of Louisiana, which would encompass the area the Spanish called Upper Louisiana. Now that position was available. When Jefferson asked Easton to consider the appointment, he quickly accepted. He immediately applied for a license to practice law in Indiana Territory, which would govern the District of Louisiana, and set out for St. Louis, the capital of the district. As soon as the new government was in place, Easton would be attorney general of "the largest land jurisdiction in the country."

By September, Rufus and Abial Easton and their three daughters were in Ste. Genevieve, Missouri. Easton attended a meeting held there on September 2 to discuss a circular that St. Louis merchant Auguste Chouteau and his friends had sent out in April, inviting delegates to a September 14 convention to consider applying for territorial status for the District of Louisiana. Moses Austin, who had developed an extensive mining operation at Mine à Breton, and Dr. Walter Fenwick of Ste. Genevieve led the meeting and urged town leaders not to send representatives to the convention. They believed the attempt to establish the District of Louisiana as a territory was simply an effort by the French founders of St. Louis, soon to be known as the French clique, to retain the privileged status they had held under the French and Spanish colonial regimes.

St. Louis was a bustling French town when Rufus Easton and his family arrived in September 1804. It had come a long way from the rudimentary trading post Pierre de Laclède de Liguest and his stepson Auguste Chouteau had established forty years earlier. The site for St. Louis had been chosen not by people seeking refuge from religious persecution or explorers hoping to discover gold, but by a merchant looking for a location to establish a trading post for his firm, Maxent, Laclède, and Company of New Orleans. Laclède had named the settlement for Louis IX, the patron saint of the reigning king of France. He did not realize that France had signed a secret treaty in 1762 ceding the territory to Spain, its ally in the Seven Years' War. The next year the Treaty of Paris ended the Seven Years' War between France and England, known as the French and Indian War in the American colonies, and England gained control of all the area east of the Mississippi River, including "The Illinois Country," which had been settled by French traders and explorers.

Laclède saw great promise in the location he had selected. He wrote, "I have found a situation where I am going to form a settlement which might become, hereafter, one of the finest cities in America—so many advantages embraced in its site, by its locality and central position." Laclède and Auguste Chouteau spent the winter of 1763-1764 in a temporary camp and trading post near Fort Chartres in the Illinois Country. In February 1764, Laclède sent Chouteau to clear the site and build the trading house. By October, Chouteau and a thirty-man crew had completed a post house and storage shed, cabins for the crew, and a large building that would serve as fur company headquarters.

Laclède himself supervised the layout of the village, patterning St. Louis after New Orleans. His design included forty blocks within the city limits. Areas for pastures and fields lay outside the city walls. A

Pierre Laclède, a partner of New Orleans merchant Gilbert Antoine Maxent, received exclusive trading rights for Upper Louisiana and the Missouri River region. He selected the site for a new frontier trading post on the west bank of the Mississippi River in December 1763 with his young stepson, Auguste Chouteau. (State Historical Society of Missouri, Columbia)

large public square adjoined the trading block, and on the opposite side of the square was the block set aside for the Catholic Church, planned to become the religious center of the settlement. Laclède platted three long streets running north and south parallel to the Mississippi River and nine short streets to provide the east-west grid of the village.

Even before the first buildings were finished, Laclède and Chouteau began their trading business at St. Louis. Curious Missouri Indians came calling while Auguste Chouteau was finishing the post house, and he set some of the Indian children and women to digging a basement in exchange for small trinkets, awls, and dyes. With the essential buildings completed before winter and a towpath prepared from the river to the post house, Laclède began encouraging native tribes to bring fur pelts to St. Louis to trade for European manufactured goods, which he had brought from New Orleans and stored at Fort Chartres. The Osage, the dominant tribe in the area, as well as the Sac, Fox, and Missouri, were accustomed to trading with French trappers and other traders who plied the rivers. They were eager to

In early 1764, Auguste Chouteau, then about fourteen years old, led a crew from Kaskaskia, where he and Laclède had spent the winter, to the site they had selected for their trading post. Laclède named the town he planned St. Louis for Louis IX, patron saint of Louis XV of France. Although France had ceded the Louisiana Territory to Spain two years earlier, word had not yet reached the colonies, and St. Louis developed as a French city, though nominally ruled by the Spanish. (State Historical Society of Missouri, Columbia)

exchange their furs for a variety of metal goods and trinkets as well as guns, gunpowder, and liquor.

As soon as the basic buildings of the trading company were completed, Laclède arranged to bring his family to St. Louis. He had been living within the company headquarters building, but he hired workmen to begin a house for his longtime companion, Madame Marie Thérèse Chouteau, her son Auguste, and the four children he had fathered with Madame Chouteau in New Orleans. Born in New Orleans in 1733, Marie Bourgeois married René Auguste Chouteau in 1749. Little is known about Chouteau, but the documents that do exist show him to have had few positive traits. Historians have found that he was identified in a slander suit, was accused of putting poison in pastries, and was abusive to his wife. Shortly after the birth of Auguste, Chouteau abandoned his family and returned to France. When Pierre Laclède met Marie, she was a young mother with no husband and no means of support. They fell in love but could not marry. Under French and Roman Catholic law, Madame Chouteau could not divorce her husband and remarry. Never explaining or

Madame Marie Thérèse Bourgeois Chouteau was born in New Orleans in 1733. Abandoned by her husband after Auguste was born, she became the companion of Pierre Laclède and came to St. Louis in September 1764 with their children. She saw her sons Auguste and Pierre become the most influential citizens in St. Louis, and she herself became a successful businesswoman after Laclède's death. (Missouri Historical Society, St. Louis)

admitting their relationship to either civil or religious authorities, Pierre Laclède and Marie Chouteau had four children together. All carried the Chouteau name.

When Madame Chouteau joined Laclède and her son Auguste in late 1764, she brought with her five-year-old Pierre, three-year-old Marie Pelagie, fifteen-month-old Marie Louise, and a newborn daughter, Victoire. In 1767 she moved into the mansion Laclède had built for her and deeded to her five children. She would spend the rest of her long and productive life there.

As the village of St. Louis grew, increasing numbers of French families moved across the Mississippi River from the Illinois Country, preferring Spanish Colonial rule to British rule. Trappers, river men, traders, and Indians were frequent visitors. Despite the availability of fertile fields and pastures nearby, the settlement continued to get most of its foodstuffs from outlying areas, especially Ste. Genevieve, which grew wheat for flour for both New Orleans and St. Louis. Trade in furs became the most significant industry, and the town quickly became identified as a fur-trading center. Laclède's own plans for trade, however, did not go smoothly. French officials revoked his firm's grant of exclusive trade. In 1765, when Laclède seized a boat of merchandise belonging to Ste. Genevieve traders on the grounds that they were violating his exclusive trading license, the courts ruled against him.

Laclède bought out his partner, Maxent, acquiring a huge debt and a valueless trading license. The number of boats stopping at the St. Louis docks in the late 1760s and 1770s indicated that a substantial amount of commerce was going on, but profits often took years to realize, and Laclède was not the only trader. While he tried to pay back debts and buy trade goods in New Orleans, Laclède gave increasing authority to Auguste, who had long ago earned his trust, and his son Pierre, still in his teens, to run the day-to-day affairs from St. Louis. The half brothers learned to survey land and chart rivers and to keep the company books. In addition, Pierre and Auguste spent a great amount of time with the Indians, Pierre often traveling to the villages of the Osage and learning their language and customs.

Pierre Laclède died suddenly in 1778 at age forty-nine, on his way back from a trip to New Orleans. He left large debts and a difficult business situation with Indian customers, especially the Osage, who had become increasingly hostile to the Spanish authorities. He also left a stepson and son capable of winning the trust of the Osage and developing the business he had founded. Auguste and Pierre Chouteau had the experience necessary to carry on the trading business and cope with the change in government. In New Orleans riots had greeted the new Spanish governor of Louisiana, but when the first Spanish lieutenant governor, Pedro Piernas, arrived in St. Louis in 1770, he was quietly welcomed. St. Louis was to remain a French town under Spanish rule, and Auguste and Pierre Chouteau were to remain its most prominent citizens.

The years the Chouteaus had spent building positive relations with the Osage paid off during the last decades of the eighteenth century. When English colonists east of the Mississippi fought for their independence from Britain during the Revolutionary War, the French west of the river stayed mostly out of the fray, independent both politically and economically from their neighbors across the Mississippi. Moreover, when British and Indian forces attacked St. Louis in 1780, the Spanish and French fended them off. Although twenty-one of the seven hundred residents of St. Louis died in the attack, the British could not convince the Osage to join them against the Spanish and French and were not able to gain a foothold on the west side of the Mississippi.

After Britain and the American colonies signed a peace treaty ending the American Revolution in 1783, the boundaries of the area the colonists had won from Britain stretched from the Atlantic Ocean to the Mississippi River but not beyond. During the next twenty years, the Chouteau brothers, with the help of their three brothers-in-law—Sylvestre Labbadie, Joseph M. Papin, and Charles Gratiot—built a remarkable fur trading and merchandising empire, acquired large Spanish land grants, accommodated themselves to changing times, and retained the trust of the Osage.

The Chouteau family's knowledge of the Indians and the Louisiana Territory became of critical importance to Meriwether Lewis and William Clark and ultimately to President Thomas Jefferson. Even before the Louisiana Purchase, Jefferson sent Lewis and Clark to explore the area west of the Mississippi, "to trace the Missouri to its source, to cross the Highlands, and follow the best water communication which offered itself from thence to the Pacific Ocean." He urged them to learn as much as they could of the Indian tribes they encountered and to bring back samples of the flora and fauna they discovered.

In December 1803, Lewis and Clark set up camp near the confluence of the Mississippi and Missouri rivers north of St. Louis. During the winter of 1803-1804, the two men frequently traveled to St. Louis as they prepared for a spring launching of their Voyage of Discovery. St. Louis stores supplied Lewis and Clark with the provisions they required for their winter camp and for their journey, and the Chouteaus provided the two leaders of the expedition with information about the Indian tribes they would encounter and the geography of the regions they would cross as they began their journey. Although Pierre and Auguste Chouteau spoke little English, and Lewis and Clark no French, the men managed to communicate, sometimes relying on Charles Gratiot or on Pierre's sons, who were bilingual. In the Chouteau homes the American explorers and the French founders of St. Louis reached an understanding. The Chouteaus, influential and knowledgeable as they were about the region and its native tribes, would do everything they could to make Lewis and Clark's expedition successful; the Americans assured their French friends that the Chouteau family would retain its esteemed position and land rights, even under American control.

In the spring of 1803, President Jefferson's representatives in Paris, Robert R. Livingston and James Monroe, opened negotiations with France to buy New Orleans and acquire shipping rights on the Mississippi. Instead, the French offered to sell all of the Louisiana Territory to the United States. Originally claimed for his king in 1682 by the French explorer René Robert Cavelier, sieur de La Salle, the vast territory reached west from the Mississippi River to the Rocky Mountains and beyond, doubling the size of the United States.

The new American authorities in New Orleans sent Captain Amos Stoddard to take possession of the northern part of the newly acquired territory and to serve as acting governor until a permanent governor could be named. Although Spain had ceded Louisiana back to France on October 1, 1800, the formal transfer had not yet taken place. In order to save money, the French charged Stoddard with also transferring Upper Louisiana from Spain to France. In ceremonies held in St. Louis on March 9, 1804, Captain Stoddard formally received the Louisiana Territory for France. Carlos Dehault Delassus delivered the territory for Spain. The Spanish flag was brought down, and the French flag was raised.

On the following day, March 10, Captain Stoddard lowered the French Tricolor and sent up the Stars and Stripes. Stoddard, with Charles Gratiot interpreting for the tearful French crowd, announced that the people were now "divested of the character of subjects, and clothed with that of citizens. You now form an integral part of a great community, the powers of whose government are circumscribed and defined by charter, and the liberty of the citizen extended and secured." He assured the French that one of the first objectives of the United States government would be to "ascertain and confirm your land titles," a matter in which Rufus Easton would soon take an interest.

Even though most residents of St. Louis wished to remain under French rule, they celebrated the raising of the American flag with a public dinner and a ball in Stoddard's honor. It was a Saturday, and according to the French custom long noted by travelers, the celebration went on for most of the night and continued after Mass on Sunday. Stoddard appreciated the warm welcome and reciprocated a month later. On Saturday, April 7, he hosted a dinner and a ball to

In March 1804 the formal transfer of Upper Louisiana from Spain back to France and from France to the United States took place at the Spanish Government House, located at Walnut and Market streets. (Mural at the George Rogers Clark Memorial in Vincennes, Indiana. National Park Service; courtesy State Historical Society of Missouri, Columbia)

which he invited Lewis and Clark as well as St. Louis leaders and many of the French townspeople. Stoddard considered his party a success but confessed his shock that the festivities had cost him $622.75, a terrifying sum for a staid New Englander.

Besides ingratiating himself with the French aristocracy of St. Louis, Captain Stoddard sought advice from the departing Spanish governor, Carlos Delassus, asking for a list of those men who had served him and could be trusted to help the United States carry out its mission of making peace with the Indians. At the top of the list Delassus provided was Pierre Chouteau, "commandant of Fort Carondelet, at the Osage Nation. . . . He is respected and feared, and I believe loved by this nation." Meriwether Lewis and William Clark reiterated Delassus's praise for Pierre Chouteau and, in fact, for the entire Chouteau clan. In order to win the goodwill of the Chouteaus for the new government, Lewis and Stoddard decided to recommend several young men of prominent French families for appointments to the prestigious military academy at West Point, which was preparing to receive its fourth class of cadets.

Military education was highly regarded by the French aristocracy, who welcomed this opportunity for their sons. On March 28, 1804, Meriwether Lewis wrote recommendations for Pierre's son, A. P. (Auguste Pierre) Chouteau; his cousin Charles Gratiot, Jr.; and Auguste Bougainville Lorimier, son of Louis Lorimier of Cape Girardeau, whose first wife, Charlotte, was Shawnee. In a follow-up letter on May 7 to Secretary of War Henry Dearborn, Captain Stoddard explained that he, too, enthusiastically endorsed the three young men as West Point candidates but expressed doubts about whether Auguste Lorimier would be accepted in the East. Stoddard had told the boy's father that at seventeen he might be considered too old for military school, but he confided that his "real objection" was that the boy "exhibited too much of the Indian in his color." He continued, "This circumstance may make his situation among the cadets at the school rather disagreeable—a situation of which he is not aware, as in this country the mixture of blood in him does not prevent his admission into the first circles." He explained that Auguste Lorimier's father was "one of the most respectable men" in the territory, but he feared that people in the East might not be quite as accepting of the young man's heritage as the French were. Stoddard's plan was for the three young men to go to Washington with Pierre

Chouteau, who had volunteered to take a delegation of Osage Indians to meet with President Jefferson.

Although Stoddard did his best to calm the nerves of the French leaders in St. Louis, they continued to worry about the American takeover. Rumors of new legislation that would affect the District of Louisiana had reached the Chouteau family. President Jefferson had, in fact, aspirations of using the Louisiana Purchase area as a republican experiment and as a place to solve some of the country's most pressing problems, especially the issues of slavery and the plight of displaced Indian tribes in the East. He had even considered a constitutional amendment that would make the region an Indian reserve, but not even his Cabinet supported that idea.

Several parts of the president's plan had, however, already been passed by Congress. Although news had not yet reached St. Louis, a bill became law just two and a half weeks after the formal transfer of the Louisiana Territory to the United States that divided the new territory in two. The area south of the thirty-third parallel was designated as the Territory of Orleans with its own territorial government, and the region north of the parallel became the District of Louisiana under the jurisdiction of Indiana Territory. Captain Stoddard, who had exercised both civil and military command of the District of Louisiana, would now serve as the civil acting commandant under the governor of Indiana Territory, William Henry Harrison, relinquishing military authority to Maj. James Bruff, who would arrive in St. Louis that summer.

The Chouteaus did not welcome having Upper Louisiana, long dominated by French families, under the control of Indiana Territory, an area less populated than their own but with increasing numbers of American settlers. Communication would be hampered not only by the distance between St. Louis and the capital of Indiana Territory in Vincennes but also by the language barrier.

Another part of the bill authorized the president to offer displaced eastern Indian tribes refuge in the District of Louisiana and discouraged further white settlement in the area. Most upsetting to the French founders of St. Louis, however, was the provision that declared all land grants issued in Upper Louisiana after October 1, 1800—the date Spain ceded Louisiana back to France but almost three years before the United States purchased the territory—to be null and void. The French had been reassured by Meriwether Lewis and Amos Stoddard that their land grants would be recognized, but now uncertainty prevailed. Another problem the French saw was the omission of any mention of slavery in the law. Although the charter for the Territory of Orleans sanctioned slavery, nothing was said relating to slavery in Upper Louisiana, causing concern among the Chouteaus and others, who had long held slaves. Rumors of possible freedom began to spread among the slaves, alarming their owners further.

Prior to learning of this bill's actual passage, worried members of the St. Louis French clique gathered to formulate a plan of opposition. Led by Auguste Chouteau, they met on April 2, 1804, and decided to convene a more general citizens' meeting on April 14. Before this meeting took place, news reached Stoddard that the bill had become law, and at the April 14 meeting French leaders decided to publish a circular and issue an invitation calling for delegates from throughout the district to convene on September 14. The purpose of the St. Louis convention would be twofold: to prepare a petition to be sent to Washington asking for the repeal of the law and submitting a request by citizens of the District of Louisiana for territorial status; and to select representatives to meet with Gov. William Henry Harrison, who announced a plan to visit St. Louis in October to launch the new government.

Meanwhile, in May 1804, Meriwether Lewis completed business matters in St. Louis, including giving Captain Stoddard power of attorney should he not return. William Clark broke camp and proceeded down the Missouri River to St. Charles, where Lewis met the expedition, and the Corps of Discovery started its long journey. A few days later, Pierre Chouteau left St. Louis with the Osage delegation, the three West Point candidates, and specimens of flora and fauna for President Jefferson.

After these historic departures, life in French St. Louis went on as before. The residents still danced, played cards, and enjoyed horse racing on Saturdays and on Sundays attended Mass and continued their "joie de vivre." As Captain Stoddard wrote his mother soon after the expeditions left: "I . . . find the French people very friendly—I even speak part of their language—and they consider it a duty as well as a pleasure to make themselves agreeable to the United States."

Nonetheless, the summer and fall of 1804 were a time of unrest for many residents of St. Louis. The French worried about the disruptions the Louisiana law might bring, and Indian leaders grew restive at the prospect of change. Perhaps most disturbing was the arrival of many Anglo Americans from the east, anxious to explore opportunities in St. Louis and farther west. The incursion of Americans with their "foreign language" and different ways began to alter the character of the French village Laclède had founded four decades earlier. As the meeting Rufus Easton had attended in Ste. Genevieve demonstrated, tensions were also intensifying between the French settlers and the American newcomers as the U. S. attempted to establish a government in its new territories.

CHAPTER 2

Life in a Hybrid Town

As the Eastons arrived in St. Louis in September 1804, their first glimpse of their new hometown was from the Mississippi River. They had traveled on a flatboat from Ste. Genevieve. Approaching the riverbank, they could see the great limestone bluff on which St. Louis was built. Some 180 stone and frame houses stood on the site, most in the style of those in New Orleans, with verandas front and back. Stone walls or high wood fences surrounded the lots. From the beginning Laclède had believed grand buildings would impress the native tribes with the power and importance of the French and would help to win their friendship.

The massive building erected for Laclède's trading post stood at the foot of la rue de la Tour, later to become Walnut Street. The building had served for a while as the Spanish government house, but Auguste Chouteau had purchased it in 1789. He transformed it into an elegant residence, adding a second floor and galleries on three sides. His house was renowned for its original polished black walnut floors, elegant furnishings, extensive library, and the hospitality of its owner. In addition to the grand residence of Madame Chouteau, other members of the French leading families, including Charles Gratiot, Sylvestre Labbadie, and Joseph Robidoux, had built mansions in the settlement, if not to impress the Indians, to provide shelter for their large families and space for entertaining.

As they drew closer to the riverbank, the Eastons would have noticed the sand towpath near the water's edge that was used to transport goods to and from the warehouses, shops, and supply houses that had grown up since the town's founding. St. Louis in 1804 was more than a fur trading post, but it was still a frontier settlement. Most of the houses were located on the two streets near-est the river. The streets were still unpaved, and not all the homes were grand. Some were log cabins, sometimes crudely finished. One of these cabins may have provided shelter for the Easton family, or Rufus Easton might have been able to rent one of the more substan-tial French houses until he could build his own. Shelter for a family was undoubtedly hard to find. Even though American merchants, agents, and vendors were crowding into the town hoping to profit from the lucrative fur trade the French had developed on the Mis-souri River, St. Louis did not yet boast a hotel.

The few businesses in town included two taverns, a bakery, three blacksmith shops, and two mills. Soulard Market, established in 1779 on land owned by surveyor Antoine Soulard, provided fresh produce and honey. New shops were springing up to cater to settlers heading farther west where the Spanish had approved land grants for a few Americans, including Daniel Boone and his family.

Around eleven hundred people, including African slaves and a few free blacks, resided in St. Louis in 1804. The majority of the white population was French, and the language was French. Not all the French were wealthy merchants. Many worked as trappers, as voya-geurs for the fur companies, or as tradesmen. A few French and Spanish officials still lingered in town, and British traders from Canada had come to explore opportunities there. Although the fam-ilies of the French founders were wealthy, Henry M. Brackenridge observed in *Views of Louisiana* that St. Louis society had "scarcely any distinction of classes." Historian James E. Davis agreed, writing in *Frontier Illinois* that in St. Louis "French, Indians, and their offspring lived, mingled freely, borrowed from each other, got along, occasion-ally spatted, and fashioned a hybrid world."

This hybrid world of mixed ethnic and socioeconomic groups was the one Mary Easton came to know, and the ability of those groups to accept one another influenced her views. She grew up in a town that on the surface at least did not discriminate against native people or those of mixed blood, although many of the French families owned slaves and depended on slave labor to maintain their way of life.

As one of the first Americans to bring his family to the French Catholic town, Rufus Easton joined other Americans in opposing the efforts of the French clique to gain territorial status for the District of Louisiana and to have the Spanish land grants confirmed. He had been promised a position as attorney general in the new District of Louisiana once the government was in place. According to William Foley, Easton was also hoping "to take advantage of the rapidly unfolding opportunities, particularly land speculation." As he had learned in Ste. Genevieve, however, the plans of the French founders of St. Louis might stand in his way. He attended the September 14 territorial convention called by Auguste Chouteau and led by Charles Gratiot. There, Easton publicly expressed his opposition to the proposed petition to Congress.

The twelve delegates attending the convention represented the subdistricts of New Madrid, Cape Girardeau, and Ste. Genevieve, as well as St. Louis and St. Charles and their dependencies. They asked for the same rights from the United States that the English colonists had demanded from the British just twenty-nine years earlier. In their "Remonstrance of the People of Louisiana," a sixteen-page document sent to Congress, the delegates declared: "Little as we are acquainted with the United States, we know by heart your declaration of independence. . . . We had anticipated the blessings of freedom." The French did not believe that the Louisiana Bill passed by Congress on March 26, 1804, had granted them those blessings. Of their twelve petitions, the most important were: recognition of the Upper Louisiana District as a self-governing territory; confirmation of Spanish land titles, including those granted after Spain ceded the Louisiana Territory back to France; and the right to "the free possession of slaves." Attesting to their allegiance to their new country in the presence of acting commandant Amos Stoddard, they swore "to be faithful to the United States, to maintain with all our power the Constitution of the United States, and to obey the laws made and to be made by Congress for the district of Louisiana."

The law establishing the District of Louisiana went into effect on October 1, 1804, and the new government took control. The five subdistricts were those the Spanish government had established: St. Charles, St. Louis, Ste. Genevieve, New Madrid, and Cape Girardeau. Each subdistrict had its own courts and justices of the peace, and Rufus Easton was to serve as attorney general of the district.

On October 3, 1804, two days after the government of the District of Louisiana went into effect, Pierre Chouteau returned from Washington, D.C., with the delegation of Osage Indians he had taken to meet with President Jefferson. Based on the strong recommendation he had received from Meriwether Lewis, Jefferson had appointed Chouteau "Agent of Indian Affairs for the district of Upper Louisiana" with a $1,500 annual salary. He charged Chouteau with the special responsibility of working with the Osage Nation. Jefferson declined, however, to grant Chouteau the exclusive trading arrangement with the Osage he had sought. The president hoped to change the Osage and other hunting and warring Indians into farmers who would live peaceably with settlers moving into the Louisiana Territory. Chouteau's long experience with the Osage and other tribes along the Missouri and Mississippi rivers led him to believe that changing their traditional way of life would be impossible, but he did not argue.

Both President Jefferson and Secretary of War Henry Dearborn assured Chouteau and the Osage of the friendship of the United States. Dearborn also promised the Osage delegation:

> All lands belonging to you, lying within the territory of the United States, shall be and remain the property of your nation, unless you shall voluntarily relinquish or dispose of the same. And all persons citizens of the United States are hereby forbidden to disturb you or your nation in the quiet possession of said lands.

After meeting with dignitaries in Washington, Chouteau and the Osage had visited several eastern cities, including New York, Baltimore, and Philadelphia. Easterners were awed by the grandeur of the Osage, led by Cheveux Blancs (White Hair), in full tribal regalia, and the Osage enjoyed the food and wine their hosts served and the displays of American naval and military might staged to impress them. Both the Osage and Chouteau returned to St. Louis in triumph. The new government had recognized the need to maintain the friendship of the Indians and had realized that Pierre Chouteau could play an important role in keeping the peace.

With other children, Mary Easton may have watched the Osage as they made their way through St. Louis to return to their villages. Following the excitement generated by the return of the Osage delegation from Washington, St. Louis was further entertained by the arrival of Gov. William Henry Harrison on October 12, 1804. Pierre Chouteau had been eager to be on hand for the planned visit and joined his half-brother in extending a warm welcome to the

Pierre Chouteau arrived in St. Louis with his mother in 1764 at the age of five and became one of the city's most prosperous traders, having received his education in "l'academie Osage." (State Historical Society of Missouri, Columbia)

territorial governor. As General Stoddard had been, Governor Harrison was impressed by the famous French hospitality and the apparent loyalty of the French to the new government. He wrote President Jefferson that "nine-tenths of the people of this Country are warmly attached to the Government of the United States."

Harrison also found Pierre Chouteau to be of great service as an Indian agent. Angered that the Osage had been invited to Washington and believing it was because the Americans feared the tribe, members of the Sac and the Fox had killed three Americans at a Cuivre River settlement, causing great alarm among settlers living nearby. Through skillful negotiations, Chouteau managed to convince the Sac and Fox leaders to come to St. Louis, where eventually Harrison got them to agree to relinquish their lands in Wisconsin, Illinois, and Missouri in return for the promise of U.S. protection, gifts, and an annual annuity. Attached to the agreement was a proviso sought by the Chouteaus that any Spanish land grants in the ceded area would be honored. Pierre's success in handling the crisis and Auguste Chouteau's diplomacy, as well as the wine, food, and entertainment, won the governor to their cause.

Although Harrison was won over by the spirit of cooperation shown by the French, some Americans, among them Rufus Easton, remained suspicious. According to *History of St. Charles County,* Easton attended the opening session of the Court of Common Pleas for the District of St. Charles on the first Tuesday of January 1805 in the home of Dr. Antoine Raynal, located on the site of what is now the St. Charles County courthouse. On January 17, 1805, back in St. Louis, he wrote President Jefferson, urging him to be wary of the French. Their real motives, he asserted, were "to secure confirmation of their land claims, many of which were undeniably fraudulent." Pierre Laclède had assigned the original lots in St. Louis by verbal agreement. When Capt. Louis St. Ange de Belerive, the French lieutenant governor of Louisiana, arrived in 1766, he required that land grants be recorded in the Livre Terrien, the Register of Deeds. This practice continued under Spanish rule. Now the American government was maintaining that grants made after October 1, 1800, when Spain ceded the Louisiana Territory back to France, were null and void. Although both President Jefferson and Governor Harrison understood Easton's misgivings and worried over claims of sedition in the District of Louisiana, they did not want to alienate the responsible French leaders. With the support of the president and Governor Harrison, Congress decided to redress some of the grievances of the new French American citizens.

On March 3, 1805, Congress passed a bill designating the District of Louisiana the Territory of Louisiana, independent of Indiana Territory, with St. Louis as the capital. Although the issue of land claims was not resolved, it was treated in a separate bill providing detailed procedures for confirmation of claims. The French felt they had achieved a qualified success with their petition.

The new territory would operate under a governor, a secretary, and three judges. On March 11, President Jefferson named the commander in chief of the army, Gen. James Wilkinson, as the first governor of the Territory of Louisiana. Rufus Easton's friend Gideon Granger applauded the selection and wrote Easton on March 16 that Wilkinson "is one of the most agreeable, best informed, most genteel, moderate, and sensible republicans in the nation." He also advised Easton: "You are to be one of the assistant judges." Jefferson also appointed Dr. Joseph Browne, Aaron Burr's brother-in-law, as secretary of the territory. Burr sent Easton a letter, praising Jefferson's

Rufus Easton arrived in St. Louis with his family in the summer of 1804. President Thomas Jefferson appointed him judge of the territorial supreme court and the first postmaster of the territory. (State Historical Society of Missouri, Columbia)

selection of both Wilkinson and Easton: "Your appointment to the office of judge of the new Territory of Louisiana gave me the utmost pleasure."

Easton was pleased to accept a seat on the territorial superior court. He also learned that he had been appointed postmaster of St. Louis. Since there had been no postal service in Spanish or French Louisiana, developing postal routes was a priority. Congress set aside funds to establish routes to St. Louis and St. Charles by extending the route from Vincennes to Kaskaskia on to St. Louis. A path had already been worn between the French towns of St. Louis and St. Charles. Called la rue de Roi, or King's Highway, the dirt road was improved for postal deliveries. Stephen Austin, the son of Easton's new friend Moses Austin, became one of the letter carriers.

Easton was also responsible for establishing a post office in St. Louis. On the first floor of the stone residence he built on Third Street, he incorporated the first post office in the settlement and also opened a law office. The family occupied the upper floors of the building. At the bicentennial celebration of the St. Louis post office, held in October 2004—although Easton had not been appointed until April 1805—former postal employee and Easton biographer

Bruce Campbell Adamson declared that Easton was the "most colorful" person in postal history next to Benjamin Franklin.

Governor Wilkinson arrived in St. Louis in July 1805, and Easton distrusted him from the start, despite the praise for the appointment he had received from Granger and Burr. Eager to introduce himself to the new governor and press his interests, Pierre Chouteau had taken a party of 160 Sac and Fox warriors down the Mississippi and met Wilkinson at Kaskaskia, managing to have a private audience with him before he met any other St. Louis supplicants. The governor considered Pierre "ambitious in the extreme" but was charmed by the cordiality of the Chouteaus. He accepted their hospitality and enjoyed the festivities they hosted to welcome him to St. Louis. The Americans questioned Wilkinson's motives for taking the job on the frontier and were dismayed by his immediate affiliation with the French clique. Historians have shown that they had good cause for their distrust. Dick Steward cites documents proving that Wilkinson had been and remained a paid agent for the Spanish, who were concerned about American expansion into the Southwest. Wilkinson had warned the Spanish of the Lewis and Clark expedition, suggesting the Spanish arrest the explorers on their way west.

Whatever his motives for accepting the position of governor and whatever his ambitions, Wilkinson set about doing the job he had been appointed to do. By the end of July he had sent Zebulon Pike to explore the headwaters of the Mississippi River and Pierre Chouteau to negotiate with the Arkansas Osage and bring representatives of the tribe back to St. Louis. The Osage would be part of a second Indian delegation to Washington requested by President Jefferson to include leaders of tribes Lewis and Clark had met on their Voyage of Discovery, who had been gathering in St. Louis since November 1804. As Indian agent, Pierre Chouteau had arranged for their housing and entertainment, and he assumed he would lead the delegation to Washington. When he returned with the Osage, however, he learned that Secretary of War Dearborn had informed Wilkinson that departing governor Amos Stoddard was to lead the delegation to the capital. This decision may have been an economic one or partly a result of questions about Chouteau's propriety in balancing his personal financial interests with his government responsibilities, or perhaps it was partly due to the influence of Rufus Easton.

Even though Gideon Granger had urged Easton to "cultivate the affection, esteem, and confidence" of Governor Wilkinson, Easton had been unable to do so. Wilkinson's favoritism toward the Old French made him unpopular with most Americans. Military commander Maj. James Bruff believed that Wilkinson had slighted him in favor of the Chouteaus. Lt. Zebulon Pike, who was back in St. Louis preparing for another western exploration, claimed that Wilkinson not only promoted the Chouteaus' commercial interests but also used his authority to favor their requests for fur-trade licenses. Soon after his arrival Wilkinson had closed the Mississippi Valley to foreign traders, ostensibly in preparation for the installation of a government trading post, but also possibly to help the Chouteaus.

In the fall of 1805 Wilkinson achieved another of his responsibilities, setting up a military outpost and Indian trading house near St. Louis. President Jefferson had asked Congress for funds to set up factories, the English term for trading posts, with the intention of winning the trust and friendship of the natives on the frontier. In 1795 Congress passed the first of a series of acts that sanctioned the factory system. Believing that competition among traders contributed to conflict among the native tribes, Jefferson's primary purpose in developing the factory system was to enable the Indians to barter for goods they needed. He thought that, in addition to regulating trade with the native people and protecting them from exploitation, the trading posts would serve as forts to provide American settlers with safe passage and prove the good intentions of the U.S. government. Congress supported the fort-trading system, and between 1796 and 1822 the United States opened twenty-eight posts. Some tribes conceded vast areas of land in exchange for trading posts and the additional services they usually offered, including a blacksmith, a milling operation, and a military garrison.

President Jefferson had charged Lewis and Clark with choosing suitable locations for factories in the Louisiana Purchase area during their Voyage of Discovery. General Wilkinson, however, chose the site for the first military outpost in Upper Louisiana, deciding it should be on the south bank of the Missouri River close to its confluence with the Mississippi. The purpose of the first fort, as Jefferson specified, was to protect the town of St. Louis and the thriving Missouri River trade as well as to provide a trading post for Indians in the area. Fort Bellefontaine was built in 1805 near the site where Lewis and

George Sibley arrived in Upper Louisiana in 1805 to serve as assistant factor at Fort Bellefontaine near St. Louis. He became factor at Fort Osage in 1808. During the War of 1812 when Fort Osage was closed, he spent time at Sibley's Post in Arrow Rock and at St. Louis. (Lindenwood University Collection, courtesy State Historical Society of Missouri, Columbia)

Clark had wintered before beginning their journey. Named for the nearby natural spring, the site also had, as Wilkinson wrote, "an abundance of timber and fuel, and a secure harbor, which circumstances are all favorable to health, convenience and economy." More than $40,000 worth of trade goods arrived in November 1805 along with two men, called factors, to manage the trading post or factory. Rudolph Tilliers was the head factor, and twenty-two-year-old George Sibley was his assistant.

Like the Eastons, Sibley had deep New England roots. His Scots-Presbyterian forebears had settled there in 1629. Restless and adventurous, various Sibleys had contributed to pushing the American frontier southward and westward, moving into western Massachusetts, western New York, the Northwest Territory, the South Atlantic and Gulf states, and the Louisiana Territory. George's father, Dr. John Sibley, distinguished himself as a physician in the Revolutionary Army and as publisher of the *Fayetteville Observer* in North Carolina. He explored the Louisiana Purchase area and in 1805 was acting as Indian agent on the western frontier of the District of New Orleans. Dr. Sibley had encouraged his son to apply for the factor's position at Fort Bellefontaine.

Born in Great Barrington, Massachusetts, in 1782, George Sibley had not had an easy childhood. While Dr. Sibley completed his service in the army, George lived with his mother; his brother, Samuel; and his mother's father, Reverend Samuel Hopkins. In 1786 Dr. Sibley moved his family to North Carolina. After the death of their mother when George was eight, the Sibley brothers lived with a family friend, Colonel Shephard, for three years. Samuel and George became very close during this time. When Dr. Sibley remarried in 1793, he enrolled his sons in school in Fayetteville and then sent them to continue their studies at the Pittsborough Academy in Chatham County, North Carolina, where George spent four years studying with the well-known Dr. William Bingham. He then studied for two more years at the Fayetteville Academy under another highly regarded teacher, Dr. David Kerr. George became well versed in literature, government, and history during those years.

When the building that housed the *Fayetteville Observer* burned in 1800, Dr. Sibley moved to New Orleans, leaving eighteen-year-old George to look after his stepmother and Samuel. During this time George worked as an apprentice under Fayetteville merchant John Winslow, who provided him with his commercial and financial education. It was this apprenticeship that best qualified George Sibley for his job at Fort Bellefontaine.

As Sibley settled into his post, his future father-in-law, Rufus Easton, was becoming increasingly disturbed by Governor Wilkinson's support of the French clique and, more important, by suspicions that Wilkinson was involved in what became known as the "Burr Conspiracy." Wilkinson's involvement in the plot seems probable, as he and Aaron Burr had several meetings in Washington during the winter of 1804-1805 before both set out for the West—Burr for New Orleans, Wilkinson for St. Louis. They had also developed a secret cipher to use in corresponding with one another.

In late August or early September 1805, just a month or so after Wilkinson took office as governor, Aaron Burr arrived in St. Louis. He later said his sole intention was to visit his new friend Rufus Easton and his longtime cohort Wilkinson. "General Wilkinson has long been my intimate friend," Burr had written Easton on March 18, 1805, just before he left Washington for his tour of the West. Some historians have come to agree, however, with President Jefferson's accusation that his former vice president's intentions were treasonous.

Jefferson believed Burr's plan included "separating the western states from us, of adding Mexico to them, and of placing himself at their head," as he later wrote.

No record of the meetings between Burr and Wilkinson in St. Louis has come to light. Easton wrote Granger that Burr called upon him, asked his opinion of Governor Wilkinson, and inquired about military officers in St. Louis who might be interested in an important venture. When Easton was not forthcoming, Burr left, promising to come back the next day, but then avoided Easton for the rest of his stay. Rumors abounded, and a century later Mary Easton Sibley's niece suggested that Jefferson had sent Easton to St. Louis to investigate Burr's western plan and report back to him. A story in a St. Charles newspaper reported that Burr disclosed his plan to Easton, and the proposal "struck him dumb and made his hair rise from his head."

Although it is unlikely that Jefferson sent Easton to St. Louis to report on Wilkinson, he might, as some historians have suggested, have sent John B. C. Lucas for that purpose. President Jefferson appointed Lucas as commissioner of land titles and to serve with Easton as territorial judge. Lucas had emigrated from France in 1784 and settled near Pittsburgh, where he had a small farm. From there, he made several trading trips west to the Mississippi River in the 1790s. He had served in the Pennsylvania legislature and had been elected to the U.S. Congress from his adopted state, but in June 1805 he, his wife, Anne Sebin Lucas, and their seven sons and one daughter boarded a government-provided flatboat and embarked on the long journey to St. Louis.

Even though Lucas was of French birth, Easton learned quickly that he was not going to become a supporter of the St. Louis French leadership. Shortly after he arrived in September, Lucas demonstrated his suspicions concerning a letter being circulated by Auguste Chouteau. As criticism of Governor Wilkinson had grown, Chouteau and other French leaders determined to compile a list of the governor's supporters. Called "The Wilkinson Memorial: A Roster of Men in the Missouri Territory, 1805," the letter did not include the name of Rufus Easton. Correspondence between Easton and Moses Austin during the fall of 1805 suggests that collusion might have occurred between them against Wilkinson. Austin wrote Easton about the "most disagreeable predicament," while Easton discredited Wilkinson for not appearing "to understand much about civil government."

Easton decided he should document his version of the story and wrote to Gideon Granger about the controversy. He reported that Wilkinson had slandered him, telling his friends, "Damn Easton, damn him, I will have no more to do with him," and had spread rumors that Easton was planning a military government with Burr. All sides had expressed righteous indignation, and Easton felt it necessary to declare his loyalty to Wilkinson.

With John B. C. Lucas's arrival in St. Louis, Rufus Easton gained an unlikely ally. Lucas wrote President Jefferson, criticizing the Chouteaus and their allies for their part in "The Wilkinson Memorial," which he saw as an attempt to save their benefactor, Wilkinson. Then, at an early meeting of the land commission, Lucas stood up to Auguste Chouteau and Julien Dubuque, casting the sole vote against their mine claims on 125,000 acres that had been part of the land relinquished by the Sac and Fox in 1804. Lucas also allied himself with Easton in protesting Governor Wilkinson's repeated interference in support of the French in their claims for title to other Spanish land grants.

William Foley wrote that the political culture of St. Louis was "intensely personal," and "individual feuds and personal grudges were the order of the day." In one example of a social event leading to violence, Easton publicly attacked James L. Donaldson. Governor Wilkinson had appointed his close friend Donaldson to serve as territorial attorney general. Both Lucas and Easton believed Donaldson to be a puppet appointed to do Wilkinson's bidding. Besides, Congress had provided only for a governor, a secretary, and three judges, not an attorney general. Therefore, the two judges refused to recognize Donaldson's commission. Donaldson, for his part, persisted in prosecuting cases. One evening at dinner at the governor's table, Easton thought Donaldson had insulted him. He considered challenging Donaldson to a duel, but his old friend Gideon Granger advised against it. "I beg you to be more of a man," Granger had cautioned, "to partake more of the divinity, and not to be driven about by every blast of folly."

Not persuaded, Easton burst into an open session of the Board of Land Commissioners when Lucas and Donaldson were presiding and struck Donaldson with a cane "at least five times," according to Dick Steward in *Duels and the Roots of Violence in Missouri*. Trying to defend himself, Donaldson reached for his "sword cane" but was

After Lewis and Clark returned from their Voyage of Discovery to the Pacific, William Clark served first as U.S. Indian Agent for tribes west of the Mississippi and then in 1813 as governor of the territory. (State Historical Society of Missouri, Columbia)

restrained. After the incident, the agent to the land commissioners, William C. Carr, felt that Easton could have handled the situation better by attacking Donaldson on the street, "where the whole community would have approved."

The summer of 1806 saw considerable activity in St. Louis as the town prepared for the return of Lewis and Clark from their two-year Voyage of Discovery. Fort Bellefontaine opened to substantial trade from residents of St. Louis, even though not as many Indians as expected made the long journey to the fort. President Jefferson decided not to reappoint Rufus Easton as territorial judge, but he kept his job as postmaster. The president also determined that the controversial governor would have to go, although his removal would be to New Orleans as military governor.

In September 1806 Lewis and Clark had spent the last night of their expedition at Bellefontaine. When they reached St. Louis, they received a warm welcome from the Chouteau family. The explorers dined with one of the brothers the first night and the next night enjoyed a ball given for them, regaling their hosts and other guests with stories of their adventures. Shortly afterward, Lewis and Clark, Pierre Chouteau, and another Indian delegation departed for

Washington, where more celebrations were planned. When Chouteau returned from Washington in 1807, he found he had been relieved of his position as Indian agent for the territory and would be responsible only for the Osage. President Jefferson had appointed William Clark to take his place, and Meriwether Lewis would be the new governor of Louisiana Territory. Until Lewis arrived back in St. Louis, Frederick Bates served as acting governor, replacing Joseph Browne, the brother-in-law of Aaron Burr, who had acted as governor briefly after Wilkinson's departure.

Despite his diminished role, Chouteau was kept busy trying to keep the increasing Indian unrest under control as Spanish agents from the Southwest and English traders from Canada attempted to gain tribal support. The Osage came to St. Louis demanding gifts that had been promised them and threatening to take up arms. Acting Governor Bates wanted to cut off U.S. protection and trade, including private trade with the Osage, although his threat to close the trading post at Fort Bellefontaine was not much of a deterrent, considering that the fort was not meeting the Indians' needs.

There were two problems with the location Governor Wilkinson had chosen for Bellefontaine. First, it was on a floodplain. This problem was remedied by moving the fort to higher ground, where it would serve as a major military installation until 1826, when Jefferson Barracks was built. Second, the trading post was not convenient for the Indians it was supposed to serve. When Osage leader Sans Oreilles visited in 1807, he told Tilliers that most of the Osage and other tribes feared risking an encounter with enemies when making the journey to the post. Bellefontaine had, however, proved convenient as a stopping-off place for expeditions headed west and as an arsenal. It was also convenient for residents of St. Louis. Bellefontaine Road, a well-worn path between the town and the fort, allowed easy socialization between the two communities.

George Sibley had his own problems at Fort Bellefontaine. After he had held his position as assistant factor for two years, Tilliers dismissed him, complaining about his self-righteous and superior attitude. Sibley was outraged about his ouster. Tilliers's careless bookkeeping had become intolerable to him, and he had been taught since childhood to speak his mind. He set off for Washington, where he told his story to the superintendent of Indian affairs, Gen. John Mason, and explained the inconvenience of the location of the fort for the Indians. Evidently he convinced Mason, who determined to close the factory at Fort Bellefontaine and move it to a new fort, which would be built on the bluffs of the Missouri River at a site near present-day Independence, Missouri, chosen by William Clark on the Voyage of Discovery.

In the summer of 1808 Meriwether Lewis, who had arrived back from Washington to take up his duties as governor of the Louisiana Territory, sent Indian Agent William Clark, then also a brigadier general in the territorial militia, with a company of eighty men to establish "Fort Clark," as it was first called. Guided by Nathan Boone, Daniel's youngest son, Clark's group of mostly volunteer dragoons set out by foot from St. Charles on August 25, 1808, to build the fort and negotiate a treaty with the Osage. When he came to the site he had previously recommended, Clark "found the River could be completely defended and Situation elegant, this Situation I had examined in the year 1804 and was delighted with it and am equally so now." Ten days earlier, Capt. Eli B. Clemson and a company of eighty-one soldiers, who would form the garrison of the fort, had embarked from Fort Bellefontaine. Of the six keelboats in the expedition, four were laden with $20,000 in trade goods purchased by George Sibley. Part of this merchandise came from Tilliers's stock, and the rest had been ordered in Pittsburgh. Sibley, who was to be factor at the new trading post, joined Captain Clemson for the trip up the Missouri to the site of the planned fort and trading post intended to serve the Osage and Kansa tribes.

After Clark had drawn up the plan for the fort and factory and set the men to work, he undertook the negotiations for a treaty with the Osage. Even though the United States had already purchased the Louisiana Territory from the French, President Jefferson believed that to keep peace with the Indian nations it was necessary to negotiate for the lands they claimed as their hunting grounds at a price that was reasonable to them. Shortly after arriving at the site in August, General Clark sent Nathan Boone and Paul Loese, the garrison interpreter, to notify the Osage of his arrival and invite them to take up residence near the fort.

Within a few days, two chiefs and seventy-five warriors arrived with all their belongings, prepared to enter into an agreement with the white men. In a treaty signed on September 14, 1808, the Osage ceded to the United States land south and east of the fort, reaching to the Arkansas

River, roughly half of present-day Missouri and a large part of Arkansas. In return the U.S. government promised to provide a trading house, mill, and blacksmith shop as well as protection for the Indians who lived within the six square miles surrounding the fort. The Big Osage were to receive an annuity of $1,000 and the Little Osage one of $500. The Osage seemed happy with the agreement and with the presents Clark gave them after the signing, including $317.74, tobacco, paint, blankets, and a gun and ammunition for the chiefs. The chiefs "touched the feather" and then used the quill to make their marks. Clark and Sibley signed the treaty, and the Osage celebrated all night and made Clark an honorary Osage, christening him Chief Red Hair.

Not only did Congress fail to ratify the treaty of September 14, but some Osage who had not been present at the signing protested that they did not understand it. Historian Jeffrey Smith, among others, believes Pierre Chouteau encouraged the Osage protest. In the treaty Clark had drawn, a parcel of land owned by Pierre Chouteau was left on the Osage side of the boundary line. In November, Meriwether Lewis wrote a new treaty that was identical to the first except that it located Chouteau's land on the American side of the line. In his report to President Jefferson, Lewis noted: "I am fully persuaded that the Indians were urged to make those objections by some white person, or persons, in this place [St. Louis], but, as I have not been able to collect any evidence of the fact, I shall avoid the mention of names. I well know that General Clarke [*sic*] would not have deceived the Indians." When Chouteau delivered the new treaty to the Osage, Sibley expressed his concern about Chouteau's role in the affair:

> Mr. Chouteau held his council on November 11th, and the Same day the Indians Signed the Treaty . . . it does not differ very materially from the one made by General Clark. . . . Mr. Chouteau concluded it in great haste and made use of threats to make the Indians Sign it. He executed it in the presence of only one Witness . . . whereas it appears on the face of it that Two other witnesses were present (Capt. Clemson & Lt. Lorimier) who in fact were not present at all, those Gentlemen Signing it merely for form's Sake, which I was invited also to do, but peremptorily Refused.

The post now became Fort Osage, but even before construction was finished Sibley set to work to establish himself as the "Little

Father" to the Indians who traded there. Despite, or perhaps because of, his frail appearance, his formal manners and dress, his fastidious attention to detail, and his insistence on a rigid schedule, George Sibley was well liked by the Indians. On September 25, 1808, Sibley wrote in his diary, "An old Osage came to me with Tears in his eyes & begged for a little blue cloth to bury his Wife in. He brought a couple of Skins to pay in part for it and Said he would pay the Rest another time." Given the man's distress, Sibley decided to let him have the cloth, and his reputation for generosity spread. He soon proved, however, that he could be firm. When the Kansa Indians arrived in October to barter with stolen goods, their "insolent and violent conduct" caused Sibley to bar them from further trading. Clark, reporting to the department of Indian affairs, noted that Sibley's policy of refusing to let the Kansa trade was having "a very good effect," as they were "becoming very humble" and had given up several horses to pay back those they had stolen.

In December 1808, Sibley wrote his brother that he had "no doubt of the Success of the establishment, so that I look with certainty for an increase of salary in the spring." During the factory's first six months of operation, it showed a gross profit of $3,700. Besides running a successful post, Sibley kept disagreements with other traders, with whom the government was not in competition, to a minimum. He also managed to get along with Pierre Chouteau, even though he had no respect for him in his dual roles as trader and Indian agent for the Osage.

The traders who passed through Fort Osage included Manuel Lisa, members of the Robidoux family, and representatives of the St. Louis Fur Trading Company and John Jacob Astor's American Fur Company. In May 1809 Meriwether Lewis sent Pierre Chouteau with 125 militiamen to escort Mandan Chief Sheke-Shote, or White Coyote, and his family back to their village in present-day North Dakota, providing $7,000 worth of goods to distribute to the Indians on the way. Lewis also authorized Chouteau to trade on behalf of the newly organized St. Louis Fur Company, whose investors included Lisa, Pierre Chouteau himself, William Clark, and Reuben Lewis, the governor's brother.

Chouteau had expected to receive accolades for having reunited Chief Sheke-Shote with his tribe, but his trip drew criticism. On his return to St. Louis he found a letter from the Madison administration refusing to approve payment of the expedition's bills, and he learned that Meriwether Lewis, whose integrity President Madison had questioned, had died on the Natchez Trace on his way to Washington to clear his name. Although Lewis's death remains a mystery, William Clark and others believed he committed suicide.

In 1809 the Chouteau family continued to dominate the Indian trade and social life, but St. Louis had changed dramatically from five years earlier. The town had been incorporated, and the street names had been changed from French to English. St. Louis even had an English-language newspaper, the *Louisiana Gazette,* later called the *Missouri Gazette.* It was the first newspaper in Louisiana Territory, started by Joseph Charless shortly after his arrival in 1808. Not all the changes were positive, however. The old French society of St. Louis had prided itself on being not only egalitarian but also hierarchical, with everyone recognizing his own place in society. The Americans who came to St. Louis in the early days after the Louisiana Purchase were of "unfixed rank." They "aggressively pursued their fortunes," according to Martha Sexton, who wrote that "violence in service of economic and political interests was common." Presbyterian minister Timothy Flint, who went to St. Louis for the first time in 1816, wrote that going beyond the Mississippi was to venture "Beyond the Sabbath." Dick Steward, in his book by that title, suggests that the era of French, Indian, and Spanish control "was by far the most peaceful in early Missouri history." Violence later became all too common on the Western frontier.

Amid these changes, the Eastons settled into life in St. Louis. Rufus maintained his position as postmaster and was earning a reputation as a lawyer. Abial Easton was busy at home with a growing family. In addition to the three daughters who had traveled from New York to St. Louis in 1804, she had a young son, Alton Rufus Easton, born January 23, 1807. While Rufus Easton was looking into land development, investments, and making his fortune, his wife was worrying about her children's education in what sometimes still seemed like a French town.

CHAPTER 3

Educating Mary

Educational opportunities for children, especially for girls, were limited when Rufus and Abial Easton arrived in St. Louis with their three young daughters. Two French schools existed in the village in 1804. Jean Baptiste Truteau had established the St. Louis School for Boys in his home in 1774, which he operated until 1824, with time off for exploration and trading expeditions. In addition to reading, writing, and arithmetic, he taught his students philosophy, literature, basic science, religion, and history with an emphasis on the ancient Greeks and Romans. A French Catholic widow, Maria Josepha Pinconneau dit Rigauche, had opened the St. Louis School for Girls in 1787 with encouragement from Spanish governor Baron de Carondelet in New Orleans. He promised to pay her fifteen pesos a month, a salary that never arrived. In lieu of the salary she finally received a Spanish land grant in 1800 but closed her school in 1805.

Even without formal French schooling, growing up in a small, close-knit French village was in itself an education for an American child. Many early travelers in the Louisiana Territory noted the French custom of including children in all social activities, including the weekly dances. The parties, often criticized by the Americans, were not "occasions for frivolity," according to Brackenridge, but "schools of manners" in which "the children of the rich and poor were placed on a footing of perfect equality."

Mary Easton became more familiar with the language and customs of the old French families through her friendship with Nancy Anne Lucas. The arrival of the Lucas family in 1805 was important to the Eastons for many reasons, one of which was that Nancy Anne and Mary became lifelong friends. The only daughter of J. B. C. and Anne

ST LOUIS RIVERFRONT ABOUT 1814

This depiction of the St. Louis riverfront about 1814 was etched on a rare bank-note discovered by Charles Peterson. (Charles van Ravenswaay Collection, State Historical Society of Missouri, Columbia)

Lucas, Nancy Anne was almost three years older than Mary. She was nearly eight in September 1805, and Mary was not yet six, but Mary knew St. Louis. She had also had an opportunity to learn about the Native American visitors to the settlement and about African proverbs and stories from slaves in the households she visited. Both girls probably spoke a mixture of French and English and were able to communicate well enough that their understanding grew. Mary showed Nancy Anne the town, introducing her to the shops, the harbor, the market, the Indians, and the French friends she had made.

Although Judge Easton and Judge Lucas may have opposed the French in court over land claims and other issues, they soon realized that they and their children were like the French founders of St. Louis in education and experience. Rufus and Abial Easton came to be regarded as part of what Frances McCurdy called "a coterie of aristocrats who exchanged social amenities with the wealthy French residents and who included in their reading the plays of Shakespeare, the essays of Hume and [Edward] Young's *Night Thoughts*." Both the

French and the Americans understood that it was in their interest to get along socially. In addition to the Chouteau family's well-deserved reputation for hospitality, Auguste Chouteau's remarkable book collection, which included English as well as French classics, must have been an attraction for the educated Americans residing in St. Louis.

After the 1804 transfer of French Louisiana to the United States, Protestant ministers could legally settle in the Louisiana District. Some began to offer classes, but many soon went farther west, following American settlement along the Missouri River. As the demand for education in St. Louis grew, a German immigrant, Christopher Schewe, opened a boys' school in 1809. He taught French, English, and German, as well as geography and mathematics, but according to William Foley, he had to sell "candles on the side" to supplement his income. Charles van Ravenswaay wrote of a young lawyer from Virginia, George Tompkins, later a justice on the Missouri Supreme Court, who tried teaching. Tompkins "offered courses in French, English, arithmetic, geometry, trigonometry, grammar and geography," but even though he took "a partner to help him, he soon gave up" and "wished the parents of his students 'luck in securing a better man.'" When parents urged him to reconsider, he sold all his educational material to show his determination to close his school.

Another venture van Ravenswaay described was that of Mme. Angelique La Grange Pescay, a native of France who opened a school for young ladies "with a practical curriculum that was far ahead of its time." He described her philosophy: "'The vicissitudes of fortune,' she said, . . . 'have taught me as well as many others, how useful it is for young persons to be early accustomed to habits of order and industry.'" Along with classes in "reading, writing, ancient history, and French grammar, she proposed to offer lessons on domestic economy and require daily supervised exercise in her orchard after dinner because that was 'necessary to health.'" She charged $140 a year, and several leading families patronized her school. However, after a few years the school failed, and Mme. Pescay was jailed for debt. Probably more popular with young ladies, as well as young men, was a dance school opened by Pierre St. Martin in September 1809. He advertised "all the new European dances (particularly the Waltz) . . . in the handsomest style."

The early nineteenth century was a time of changing attitudes about the education of women. Born in the generation after the

American Revolution, Mary Easton experienced the contradictory sentiments about women's education the Revolution produced. On the one hand, women were expected to be independent thinkers, which Mary certainly learned to be. On the other hand, next to beauty, which Mary also had, domestic skills were considered necessary for a young woman to be marriageable, and marriage was considered the only option available. For the generation of women preceding the Revolution, having book learning had not been considered necessary, or even desirable, for a girl. By the early 1800s, however, sufficient book learning became a requirement to acquire a good—meaning well educated and moneyed—husband.

Psychologist Carol Gilligan concluded that women in the early republic defined their moral worth by their ability to care for and respond to the needs of their husbands and children. Education was considered essential for children of wealth, and it could best be acquired within a family structure where the work ethic was valued. Rearing a child included providing education in morals and religion as well as in reading and writing. It was only within the protected circle of the family that mothers could teach their children the virtues they needed. Especially in newly populated areas of the country where danger was ever present, the only safe place was home.

Hints of the influence her mother had on Mary Easton's education can be found in comments Mary made in the journal she kept after her religious conversion some years later. Little is known of Abial's upbringing other than that she was from a prominent Eastern family. According to Mary's remembrances, her mother loved poetry. Unlike most women of her time, she apparently was not affiliated with a church, possibly because she did not believe churchgoing promoted independent thinking. At a time when poetry had come to be regarded by some as a source of spiritual comfort and a substitute for religion, Mary's mother taught her daughter how to read verse and appreciate the sentiments and feelings it could evoke.

Prosperous residents of St. Louis could order new books from the East or from Europe, and Abial Easton introduced Mary to the works of Lord Byron, possibly to his first book of poems published in 1807, and then to *Childe Harold's Pilgrimage,* which became available in 1812. Although Byron became one of the most famous of the Romantic poets, critics of the time did not consider his poetry to be as lofty or as wholesome as that of Wordsworth and Coleridge, but

Mary continued to admire his work, especially his Faustian drama, *Manfred,* published in 1816, which she read after she married. She confessed in her journal that before her religious conversion, when she was an "unregenerated person," she was a great admirer of Lord Byron's knowledge of the human soul. In *Manfred* she found the "genius of the author, in depicting the passions and noblest affections of human nature in its natural state . . . selfishness, arrogance, pride and ambition."

Mary may also have acquired her view of the goals of education from her mother. She wrote in her journal in 1833 that girls should not become "helpless, dependent creatures, mere Doll babies . . . for exhibition decorated with external accomplishments, very pretty to hold in the Drawing room or Ball room but of no manner of use either to ourselves or their fellow creatures, when called upon to take their stations in society as wives, mothers, and heads of families. Then they need to be *practically* and *experimentally* and what is worth more than all *habitually* acquainted with all the *various duties* of Domestic economy and arrangement." Only when "this essential knowledge is combined [with] a *liberal* education do they become the pride, the comfort, the stay of their relatives and friends, whereas on the other hand they become a burden to all with whom they are connected." In accord with these sentiments, Mary's parents encouraged her to learn domestic skills, which she never enjoyed, and as the oldest daughter to tend and teach her younger siblings. She seems to have liked the teaching part.

Rufus and Abial Easton believed in giving their daughters and sons equal educational opportunities, and Mary had acquired a collection of books of her own by the time she married. She learned how to play the piano and sing, attributing her musical accomplishments to the influence of her father. Historian Duane Meyer reports that there were several pianos in St. Louis by the 1790s, and Rufus Easton gave his daughter a special one with fife-and-drum attachments some time before her marriage. There are indications of a close relationship between Rufus Easton and his firstborn. From an early age, Mary often rode with her father on errands and visits and learned about the many activities in which he was involved as a postmaster, lawyer, and then politician and land investor. As a prominent attorney and federal government official he entertained important guests—legislators, judges, entrepreneurs, and nationally known figures including

Daniel Boone, William Clark, and John Jacob Astor. From these experiences Mary learned social skills that later served her well. Her father taught her Latin, and he apparently encouraged her interest in politics.

Character, principle, and respectability were essential qualities for a girl to acquire, traits many believed were best taught at home. Staying home was probably also the safest option for the Easton children during Mary's early school years. Real dangers brewed around St. Louis. Clashes between American upstarts and the French founding families seemed less important as Native American tribes fought with one another over hunting lands and grew more resentful of American settlers. As relations between Britain and the United States grew increasingly strained, war seemed imminent. President Jefferson had tried "peaceful coercion" by urging Congress to pass the Embargo Act, forbidding all land and seaborne commerce with foreign nations, which turned out to be an economic disaster for the United States.

A group in Congress known as the War Hawks clamored for a declaration of war, and President Madison, who took office in March 1809, seemed to be on the Hawks' side. Rumors of British collusion with the Indians brought panic to the Louisiana Territory. The territory seemed less prepared for war than the rest of the country for both political and military reasons. William Clark had reported that western defenses were extremely fragile as militiamen were unarmed and widely scattered. St. Louis seemed especially vulnerable, a sure target for British and Indian forces should war come. Fort Bellefontaine could hardly be expected to offer protection to such a large area.

After Meriwether Lewis's death, President Madison offered the governorship of the Louisiana Territory first to William Clark and then to Frederick Bates, who had served briefly after Wilkinson's departure. When both declined, Madison appointed Benjamin Howard, a Kentuckian, who accepted the post in April 1810 but did not arrive in St. Louis until September. By that time, the Osage had become especially disruptive. William Foley suggests that the 1809 death of Pawhuska (Cheveux Blancs or White Hair), an Osage leader and a longtime friend of the Chouteau family, had led to increased tension between the Little and Big Osage. In addition, both factions of the tribe felt that the U.S. government and Chouteau had deceived and misled them. In the spring of 1811 the Osage nation complained to Pierre Chouteau and to George Sibley about neglect, and Chouteau's barn was burned, an act he blamed on the Osage. Congress had failed to ratify either version of the treaty of 1808 and had not paid the promised annuities. Finally, with much urging from the governor, Sibley, and Chouteau, Congress ratified the treaty with the Osage in July 1811 and authorized the money to provide the Osage with a corn mill, a forge, and their annuities.

Other Indian tribes rebelled as well, mostly against each other. President Jefferson had invited some eastern tribes to settle west of the Mississippi, including Cherokees and Shawnees, threatening to displace the tribes already there. Rumors of a possible Winnebago attack against Fort Bellefontaine put St. Louis on alert, and Potawatomis killed two white men near the town in June 1811. A month later the Ottawas threatened Pierre Chouteau's life. Governor Howard ordered the construction of blockhouses at strategic locations and asked Auguste Chouteau to ready St. Louis for attack from the Indians, the British, or both. Stories of "Redcoats" seen in Indian villages were common. St. Louis residents, including the Eastons, were nervous.

Meanwhile, as fears of violence increased in St. Louis, up the Missouri River at Fort Osage the Indians were calm and travelers continued to make stops. Manuel Lisa, a St. Louis merchant and trader, founder of the St. Louis Fur Company with William Clark, Auguste and Pierre Chouteau, and others, stopped there in the late spring of 1811.

During the spring of 1811, Sibley, intrigued by the stories various explorers and traders brought to the fort, decided to undertake an expedition west himself. Sans Oreilles, a Little Osage leader, accompanied him on the two-month journey. Called "No Ears" by the French because he would not listen to advice, Sans Oreilles had become friends with "Chief Red Hair" and Sibley. With two Osage warriors to serve as scouts, a hostler, an interpreter, and two Osage on their way to their villages, Sibley visited the villages of the Big and Little Osage, the Kansa, and the Pawnee.

Sibley also wanted to see the rumored "salt mountain," a description that intrigued former president Jefferson. Osage guides knew of the Great Salt Plains in present-day northwest Oklahoma, as many wars had been waged and many treaties made over the control of the salt. The first white man known to have seen the site, Sibley described it as a "perfectly level plain, covered in dry hot weather from 2 to 6 inches deep with beautiful clean white Salt, of a quality rather Superior I think to the imported Brown Salt." He reported to Clark that he had dug out a piece of salt "16 inches thick," much to the amusement of an Indian, who asked him if he "expected to dig to the bottom."

Though visitors to Fort Osage were declining, after his return Sibley continued to report to Clark on those who came. The winter of 1811 to 1812 must have been a time of great worry for the Easton family, as well as other residents of St. Louis, as the possibility of war with England increased. To add to the unrest, townspeople woke early on the morning of February 7, 1812, to a great vibration. According to the February 8 edition of St. Louis's *Louisiana Gazette,* "On Thursday morning last, between 2 & 3 o'clock, we experienced the most severe shock of earthquake that we have yet felt, many houses were injured, and several chimneys thrown down; few hours pass without feeling slight vibrations of the earth." St. Louis had experienced the reverberations from an earthquake on the New Madrid fault, the largest ever recorded in the contiguous United States. Preceded by two other major quakes on December 16, 1811, and January 23, 1812, the February 7 quake destroyed about half of the town of New Madrid and was felt strongly over fifty thousand square miles. Scientists have since determined that the quake had a magnitude of about 8.0 on the Richter scale. The effects included changes in the course of the Mississippi River, which actually ran backward for a short time. Continued vibrations from inside the earth kept the residents of St. Louis on edge for the rest of the winter of 1812.

Despite the earthquake and the fear of war, the population of St. Louis had increased modestly to 1,400 people with twelve stores, two private schools, and a printing office. Meanwhile, the white population of the Louisiana Territory had doubled between 1804 and 1810 from 10,000 to 20,000. In June 1812 Congress created the Missouri Territory, renaming the former upper Louisiana Territory to distinguish it from the new state of Louisiana. William Clark became the new territorial governor. As a second-class territory, Missouri now had the right to have its own popularly elected legislative and judicial branches and to send a representative to Congress. Some believed Missouri Territory was just a step away from statehood, but that step was delayed by another event of 1812. On June 18, the United States declared war on Great Britain. Word reached St. Louis that the Shawnee, Kickapoo, Potawatomi, Winnebago, and Miami nations had agreed to join the British in waging war against the United States.

St. Louis prepared for the worst. A seven-person committee of safety led by Auguste Chouteau supervised construction of fortifications and organized the town's defenses. Pierre Chouteau journeyed to the Osage villages to reassure the Osage and try to keep their loyalty. William Clark reported to Secretary of War James Monroe that Pierre Chouteau's role with the Osage was invaluable. However, others, including Rufus Easton and George Sibley, questioned his motives. Easton had always been suspicious that the Chouteaus were motivated mainly by monetary interests. When Pierre wanted to close the trading factory at Fort Osage in 1813, Sibley believed it was because it competed with Chouteau's own business activities. Even though the Osage offered Sibley their help to defend the post, the government determined to close it because of its isolated and presumably indefensible position.

Dejected, Sibley retreated to St. Louis with his goods, but he approached Clark about establishing another trading post for the Osage. Sibley argued that in the treaty of 1808 the Osage had been guaranteed a trading post and a blacksmith, in partial compensation for land they had given up in Missouri and Arkansas. These promises needed to be kept, Sibley believed, to maintain friendly relations with the Osage and also to keep the British from establishing their own profitable trade with the Indians. Finally, Clark agreed to allow Sibley to construct a temporary trading post on the Missouri River near present-day Arrow Rock. At the same time, he authorized a second post to be set up on the Little Moniteau River, near present-day Jefferson City, to accommodate the Sac Indians. Later, a third post opened near Glasgow for the Ioways.

Although frontier settlements around St. Louis were attacked and the American post at Prairie du Chien fell to combined British and Indian attack, St. Louis did not come under fire during the War of 1812. Local records, however, including the census of 1810, were reportedly lost. Although the war ended in December 1814 with the Treaty of Ghent, word had not reached the United States when the Battle of New Orleans was fought on January 8, 1815. Although peace negotiations with the hostile tribes did not occur until later,

German immigrant Gert Goebel reported that the Indians knew before word reached the St. Louis area that the British had lost in New Orleans and began to leave quietly.

The Treaties of Portage des Sioux, signed by leaders of eleven tribes between July 18 and September 16, 1815, settled the Native American and U.S. conflict and also affirmed both the Treaty of St. Louis of 1804, when the Sac and Fox had ceded land in what is now northeast Missouri, Illinois, and Wisconsin, and the 1808 Treaty of Fort Clark, in which the Osage ceded their lands in Missouri and Arkansas.

During these peace conferences, Rufus Easton was in Washington, D.C. Elected on September 17, 1814, to serve as the second Missouri Territory delegate to the U.S. Congress, Easton introduced important legislation. He proposed Missouri statehood and sponsored an act to reform land claims that remained entangled after the Louisiana Purchase. He introduced a bill to give veterans of the War of 1812 land grants as well as pay them pensions. Another bill passed by Congress, entitled "Relief of the Inhabitants of the late county of New Madrid, who suffered by earthquakes," written by Clark in January 1814 and submitted by Easton, was possibly the first plea ever made for federal disaster relief.

Easton may have taken Mary to school on his way to Washington in the fall of 1814. It is uncertain when Mary went away to school, but the Eastons had concluded she could not get the education she needed in St. Louis and decided to send her to a boarding school in Kentucky. Mary's great-niece remembered that Mary had told her that "the only means whatever to get there was on horseback to Washington, D.C., and back again." Equally uncertain is which boarding school she attended. In her centennial address to Lindenwood College, Lucinda de Leftwich Templin repeated what Mary's great-niece had told her, that Mary "was sent to the only seminary for women in the West, Mrs. Tevis's Boarding School for Young Ladies, at Shelbyville, Kentucky." Many histories, articles, and dissertations have perpetuated this misinformation, until it has become part of the Mary Sibley lore.

If Julia Ann Hieronymus Tevis's Science Hill Female Academy had been open when Mary Easton's parents were looking for a school for their daughter, it would have been a likely place to send her. For more than a century, Science Hill Academy was a highly respected college preparatory school for young ladies, and Julia Ann Hieronymus was considered a brilliant teacher. However, Mrs. Tevis's school was not opened until 1825, and Mary Easton probably attended a boarding school in Kentucky when she was fourteen or fifteen, sometime between 1813 and her marriage in 1815.

The school that Mary Easton attended was most likely the Shelbyville Female Academy in Lexington. Both the town of Shelbyville and Shelbyville School were named after Isaac Shelby, elected the first governor of the state of Kentucky in 1792. Shelbyville Female Academy, also called Shelby College, was chartered by the Kentucky General Assembly in December 1798 and remained in operation until 1868. Therefore, it would have been an option for Mary Easton. The Shelbyville Female Academy was billed as a "Select Institution for Young Ladies" by its founders, who were from Philadelphia, the city where the earliest schools dedicated to female education began. Edward Barry and his wife wanted to foster in young ladies a lifelong love of learning without rote memory and recitation. The use of "the inductive method," they said, "will be studiously observed, and instruction conveyed by explanations and illustrations."

According to William Starr Easton's family genealogy, published in 1899, Mary Easton Sibley "received a liberal education, attending a female institution in Lexington, Kentucky," known as the "Athens of the West," "to which place and back to St. Louis she made the journey on Horseback." If Mary Sibley did not attend the Shelbyville Female Academy in Lexington, she could have been enrolled at a second Lexington girls' school that also opened in 1798, Mentelles for Young Ladies. Founded by Charlotte Victorie Leclere Mentelle and her husband, Augustus Waldermarle Mentelle, who had escaped from Paris during the French Revolution, the French school opened as an adjunct of the Transylvania Seminary. The Mentelles' school was expanded in 1805 when land was donated to support the female academy by Mary Owen Russell, the great-aunt of Mary Todd Lincoln. Whether Mary attended the Mentelles' school or the Shelbyville Female Academy, she would have received instruction in the domestic, moral, and academic subjects considered appropriate by finishing schools of the era.

After one or two years of boarding school, Mary, a polished and "finished" young lady, was back home in St. Louis by the summer of 1815 and had met George Sibley. The construction of the factory and fortifications at Arrow Rock, which Clark had agreed to allow Sibley to build, began in August 1813 and was completed in October. Although Sibley's Post, as it was named, would never be occupied by military troops, it was constructed "affording sufficient room for the goods, for Trading and for fighting," Sibley wrote. The Little Osage opposed the change in location, but the Big Osage felt the new fort was safer for them. As the War of 1812 dragged on and as Indian hostilities increased, the government decided to close Sibley's Post in May 1814. Sibley did not abandon it but still met there with leaders from both the Big and Little Osage tribes. He assured them the government would pass a new trading house law that would permit the return of the factory to Fort Osage by the war's end.

Rufus Easton and George Sibley were destined to meet in a town as small as St. Louis. They also had much in common. They were both government employees and men of education, had eastern backgrounds, and were from old American families. Although George was eight years younger than Rufus, they were basically contemporaries and certainly closer in age than were Mary and George. They would learn that they shared common ideas concerning politics and the French clique of St. Louis. They also both had an interest in land speculation, as did all Americans with a little money who had ventured to the frontier.

In 1815, Rufus Easton purchased land east of the Mississippi River and laid out a town in honor of his firstborn son, Alton Rufus Easton. At the juncture of the Mississippi and Missouri rivers and near the site of the camp where Lewis and Clark prepared for their Voyage of Discovery, Alton, Illinois, recognizes Rufus Easton as its founder. The Easton family is memorialized in a Rufus Easton Street and streets named for several Easton children, Alby, Henry, George, and Langdon. However, Rufus Easton's heavy speculation in Alton, Illinois, never paid off, leaving him in "straitened circumstances for the rest of his life." George Sibley was not much luckier with his investments. Records show that by 1813 Sibley had purchased three parcels of land in and around St. Louis and St. Charles totaling one thousand acres. He expected an excellent return on his investments, "for it is morally certain," he wrote to his brother, "that as Soon as the War [of 1812] is over, the emigration to this Territory will be immense, which will you know enhance the value of land very much."

Having established himself as a man of accomplishments with landed interests and a government position, George Sibley was ready to propose to a "certain fair one, whose beauty, amiable disposition, and elegant accomplishments would adorn a palace." George and Mary must have had a courtship of sorts, but we know none of the details. If they met in Abial and Rufus's dining room, it is easy to imagine George falling in love at the sight of the pretty Miss Easton. In an early portrait of Mary, her long dark hair is pulled up, and curls frame her face and fall down her neck. Her features are delicate, and she holds herself erect. According to the story of the evening they met in 1814, George had eyes only for Mary, and no one seemed to object that she was only fourteen years old and he was thirty-two.

Mary was described by friends and family as happy, healthy, and full of spirit. Mary's great-niece Louise Gibson Conn remembered:

> Mary Easton and Nancy Lucas were considered the belles of the village. Both girls were very gay and full of health and spirits. They used to go to the dances at the surrounding forts, which were the points of interest, and I have heard Aunt Mary say that they often rode all day on horseback, with their party-clothes in a bundle behind them, and then danced all night and came back the next day. They thought nothing of physical exertion.

At twelve, thirteen, and fourteen, Mary and Nancy Anne rode horseback to forts under what would now be considered dangerous conditions, but life on the frontier was different. Although Mary later said she had first met George Sibley at a dinner party at her parents' house, it is possible that Nancy Lucas and Mary Easton met their husbands-to-be at one of these dances. In 1814 Nancy Anne Lucas married Captain Theodore Hunt, a naval commander sixteen years her senior; the next year, Mary married George Champlin Sibley. Nancy Lucas Hunt settled in St. Louis, where her husband became a partner in Manuel Lisa's fur trade business, and the two friends would cross paths occasionally in the years following their marriages until their deaths, just one year apart.

Mary and Nancy Anne loved parties and dances, a fact that did not change after Mary married George. In writing her father in Washington shortly after her marriage, Mary devoted almost half of her letter to describing the St. Louis social life:

> Our great Town has been lively enough this winter if Balls would make it so; in the first place, three at Mr. Garnier's. Mr. Carr gave a

very splendid Party; it is a wonder he did not wait till the Legislature were convened, that he might have the honor of that great body being present, for it was only a week before,—next five assembly Balls at Mr. Peebles, who keeps tavern where Mr. Austin formerly did; besides which the balls of the second class are highly celebrated.

She went on to tell about a party at Mr. Sollomon's where everyone had to pay a dollar and a half to be admitted, which Mary felt sure would make Mr. Sollomon rich. In Mary's eyes, the "democratic" society of St. Louis certainly had its social classes.

Mary met George when she was fourteen, and at fifteen she was considered to be of marriageable age. She also was considered old enough not to be doing such "unladylike" things as crossing her feet in public, galloping on horseback, or slumping in her chair; yet Mary did unladylike things anyway. As described in *The Linden Leaves* of 1923, Mary lost none of her "sturdy vitality" when she became Mrs. Sibley, "nor did she for once consider settling down." George liked her vivaciousness and recognized her many talents. Even though, as Alexis de Tocqueville noted in *Democracy in America,* "In America, the independence of women is irrevocably lost in the bonds of matrimony," Mary Easton, raised to think for herself, did not lose that free spirit once she became Mary Sibley.

Mary could play the piano, write a beautiful hand, teach children how to read and write, and carry on an intelligent conversation in English or French. She probably knew as much if not more than George did about the Indians native to Missouri, as she had grown up among them. She had been taught something about both politics and the law by her father. She had an appreciation for poetry and literature, thanks to her mother. Although household chores did not amuse her, Mary knew how to keep house, how to cook, and how to sew. When George looked at Mary Easton, he would have seen all the qualities he needed in a wife to live with him in what was then called "the howling wilderness."

George Sibley was a good match for Mary. He was well educated, had a good job, held property, and had political and social views that matched those of her father. But their relationship seems to have been a love match from the beginning and throughout their many years together, as shown by the devotion they expressed to each the other in

Mary Smith Easton married George Sibley in 1815 at age fifteen and soon moved with him to the isolated trading post at Fort Osage in present-day Jackson County. (Lindenwood University Collection, courtesy State Historical Society of Missouri, Columbia)

their letters and journals. The beautiful Mary found George to be handsome. Thin and small-boned, George appeared somewhat frail to others. However, he was known to be able to get what he wanted without raising his voice. He may have had a small frame, but he possessed a commanding presence. He, like his wife, knew his own mind.

In 1815, George Sibley was in Brownsville, Pennsylvania, awaiting the passage of the new factory bill and getting a barge fitted to transport himself and his stores of goods to St. Louis and then on to reopen Fort Osage. He wrote his brother, Samuel, who was in Natchitoches:

> I do not mean to remain long in the Indian country. I propose in about two years to commence the dry goods and Indian trade business at St. Louis on a pretty extensive scale, in partnership with an old friend of mine, a wholesale merchant of Baltimore. Something may happen, however, very advantageous to me in the public service. So you see, I have two strings to my bow.

Besides his business objectives, George revealed his marital plans to his brother: "The matrimonial connection which I expect soon to form will inevitably fix my residence in the Missouri Territory." He confided his intention to "build large and comfortable houses" at Fort Osage and "have everything secure about me." All these plans would be necessary because, as George added, "My calculations at present are to take a certain fair one with me."

Rufus Easton approved the match, and on August 19, 1815, fifteen-year-old Mary Smith Easton married thirty-three-year-old George Champlin Sibley in St. Louis, Missouri, at the home of the bride's parents.

CHAPTER 4

"A Marvelous Little Wren"

On August 20, 1815, the day after his wedding, George Sibley wrote his brother, his father, and "all others interested" of his marriage to Mary Easton. He began by admitting that he had not written to Samuel since May, as "Nothing has occurred here since then enough of importance to justify my writing you (until last night)." After telling Samuel that Indian affairs were still in an unsettled state and other news, he finally came to the point: "You must know . . . that I was married yesterday evening at 7 p.m. to Miss Mary Smith Easton, the eldest daughter of the Hon. Rufus Easton of this place. Her fortune I know nothing about, I never inquired. Her father is reckoned very wealthy. He has seven children and every prospect of having as many more." George added, "I anticipate the question from you all, 'Do you intend to take this charming wife with you among the Indians?' Yes. She has long ago expressed her willingness to live anywhere with me. Until I can withdraw from the Indian service she will willingly share with me the privations of a forest life. She will be 16 next Jan."

Sibley anticipated staying in St. Louis until spring, awaiting instructions from the Indian department about his return to Fort Osage. Although Congress had passed a new trading house law on May 6, 1815, Sibley did not want to resume trade at the factory or risk taking his bride there until the garrison returned to the fort. As he told his brother, he was loathe to live at Fort Osage "without a competent military force to protect my establishment from the predatory parties of the hostile tribes that will infest the Missouri where I shall be obliged to pass, and that part of the Osage country where I propose to locate myself." He and Mary traveled to Fort

FORT OSAGE - 1808 - JACKSON COUNTY

Fort Osage stood high above the Missouri River in present-day Jackson County, and Mary invited all passersby to stop at her home, Fountain Cottage. (Missouri State Capitol mural by William Knox, photo by Hammond and Irwin, Jefferson City, Mo., courtesy State Historical Society of Missouri, Columbia)

Osage by boat in October to move her many possessions there. But it was not until April 1816 that Mary moved from her parents' home in St. Louis and with her husband became part of the second phase of Fort Osage history.

Approximately three hundred miles west by river from Fort Bellefontaine, Fort Osage sat atop a seventy-foot embankment. The site allowed a view in both directions of the Missouri River, which narrowed along the limestone promontory. A swift current ran on the north side and in the middle of the river; boats were thus forced to navigate through the quiet water of the eddy below the cliff on the south side of the Missouri. As William Clark had realized when he chose the location, its physical attributes allowed the fort to act as a "frontier Gibraltar," as Kate Gregg wrote.

By the time he decided to wed Mary Easton and take her to Fort Osage, George Sibley had established himself as an explorer, an Indian agent, a land investor, a gifted letter writer, a loyal servant of the U.S. government, and a great asset to the Indian factory system. Clark thought of him as his "right hand," and Sibley had at least indirect, if not direct, contact with the president of the United States. He had built strong relationships with the tribes, the local settlers, and the traders and travelers on the Missouri River. Therefore, he felt sure that Mary would be as safe and comfortable at Fort Osage as in St. Louis. As George told his family, "I have had the singular good fortune to obtain a young lady to be my friend and companion through life who will not deceive my hopes of happiness."

The bride herself seemed not a bit disconcerted about the move. After all, she was not leaving behind all the comforts of home; she was taking them with her. When the Sibleys left St. Louis on October 1, 1815, for the monthlong river journey to move Mary's possessions to Fort Osage, they were accompanied by her books, her furniture, her wardrobe (although she wisely left most of her silks and satins behind), her saddle horse, and her piano with its fife-and-drum attachments. Although various accounts suggest that six keelboats or fifteen keelboats or even an "entire fleet" of keelboats was necessary to transport all of Mary Sibley's goods, those reports must have been exaggerated, as a keelboat could hold ten to twenty tons of cargo. At least one entire keelboat, however, was loaded with the essentials for the civilized life Mary Easton Sibley planned to have at Fort Osage.

After her safe arrival at Fort Osage, Mary wrote to her father: "We could only go about four or five miles a day because of the current. The banks of the Missouri are covered with timber. Occasionally an Indian would shoot an arrow from behind a tree, but never hit us. We never saw a white settler from the time we left until we got within a mile of the fort." Although this account could not have been very comforting to her father, Mary was undaunted about the journey or what lay ahead. As she continued, "Although our trip in our big, roomy flat boat up the Missouri was fraught with danger and excitement and discomforts, it was fascinating to me and I shall never forget it. As you know, I am only fifteen and very fond of adventure." Mary's first glance of her new home was at sunset. Rounding the bend in the river, she saw the high log stockade and the fort sitting prominently against the wooded bluff overlooking the Missouri River, the river near which she would spend the rest of her long life.

After moving Mary's belongings into their new house, Mary and George returned to St. Louis for the winter. There they participated in the active social life of the city, attending balls and other functions and keeping Abial Easton company while Rufus was still in Washington as a congressional delegate from Missouri Territory.

Mary wrote her father again on February 11, 1816, to scold him for his lack of communication:

> Dear Father, I will write to you (however great my aversion to let-
> ter writing) for I see plainly you have determined to try me, or else
> you would surely have given me some kind advice, as you were used
> to do when absent, & also would have desired me ere you departed,
> "not to forget to write you often," but I suppose *you think,* it is as
> much as I can do to attend to the *wise lessons* of a *husband,* if you
> do, I assure you; you are mistaken, but even supposing it were so,
> my dear Father might at least have sent me a line, to say he did not
> forget I was still in existence . . . I hope my dear Father you will
> write me a few lines, if you have not leisure for more. Your affec-
> tionate, Mary S. Easton Sibley

Mary also informed her father that the legislature was in session and that her youngest brother, Langdon, had begun to talk. George Sibley added a postscript. "I set off in a few days (by land) for F. Osage, Shall be down again in April—Pray write me if anything occurs interesting respecting Indian Affairs." Sibley also hoped that Rufus would "try and keep the British Canada Traders out of our Country by Law," as he feared that, with the end of the War of 1812, British traders would begin to compete with the government trading houses.

When Sibley returned to Fort Osage in April, he took Mary, and she brought along her twelve-year-old sister Louisa. The garrison had returned to the fort, offering safety and support for the factor and his wife. The next seven years at Fort Osage were very unlike the first phase of the fort's existence. Not many Indians lived at or near the fort after the War of 1812. Most of the Big Osage had moved closer to their homeland on the Marais des Cygnes River, while the Little Osage camped farther south in present-day Arkansas. Friction had increased between the Osage and eastern tribes, especially the Cherokee, who had begun to move west and settle onto government lands given up by the Osage, making travel to the fort hazardous. Indian trade at all government posts decreased markedly after the war, but especially at Fort Osage, due to Indian conflicts as well as to increased competition, both with long-established traders like the Chouteaus and with the Canadians, as Sibley had feared.

Mary and George Sibley began their forty-eight years of marriage in Fountain Cottage, the first house built outside the palisades of the fort in what would become the town of Sibley in Jackson County, Missouri. The house George had built was quite large for an outpost. It cost $3,000 and, according to former Lindenwood archivist Mary E. Ambler, contained twenty windows and doors. This account, however, disagrees with that of Independence, Missouri, historian Rhoda Wooldridge, who wrote that "Mr. Sibley took unusual precautions" in building a home for his new bride; the house had only one door, which faced the trail, and no windows. However, both Ambler and Wooldridge agree that Fountain Cottage was a comfortable house with fine gardens. Although Mary was never very domestic, she knew how to make her surroundings attractive. The Sibley home became the model of pioneer culture and even elegance, according to visitors. Plenty of flowers soon graced the cottage. With her fondness for bright colors, Mary chose red geraniums, which became her personal trademark. She also planted a vegetable garden, saw that the pigs were fenced in, had an icehouse built, and requested a henhouse in order to have chickens and fresh eggs. George wrote to his brother in July 1816 that "my wife seems much pleased and quite content; our quarters are very comfortable, and with the aid of very fine gardens, a well stocked poultry yard and an ice house, we are enabled to live very well."

It took only a short time for Mary Easton Sibley to make a name for herself among the Indians and with the visitors who landed at the dock at Fort Osage. Her reputation as a hostess was such that, nearly a century after she had died, she was included as a character in *Centennial*, a novel about the West written by James A. Michener and published in 1974:

> Then Mrs. Sibley appeared, a marvelous little wren dressed in a frail white dress gathered high beneath her breasts, with pink satin slippers on her tiny feet and a pale-blue ribbon in her hair. . . . She sat at the piano, adjusted her shimmering dress, turned and bowed to the Indians. This so pleased them that they made varied sounds of greeting, whereupon she started playing in dainty fashion a Mozart gigue which had floated up the river from New Orleans. . . . Mary Sibley launched into a livelier tune, and with her left foot, in a most unladylike fashion, began kicking an extra pedal, which activated a large bass drum hidden in the rear of the piano. A French dance resulted, with the drum pretty well drowning out the music. As the Indians cheered, fragile Mrs. Sibley began pumping

bellows with her right knee, activating a hidden wind instrument which played "Yankee Doodle Dandy"—and what with the booming drum and all of her ten fingers banging the keys as hard and as fast as possible, a veritable explosion of noise filled the salon.

Although this description is undoubtedly apocryphal, several accounts suggest that Mary's piano was popular with the Indians. In fact, George Sibley wrote to his brother about his wife: "Mary amuses me and herself everyday for an hour or so with her piano on which she performs extremely well. . . . You may be sure that Mary is a very great favorite among the Indians. Indeed they literally idolize her since they have seen her play." Mary's piano and her books brought culture to the fort and allowed her to become both a popular hostess and an educator.

With the Indians no longer required to live within the six square miles surrounding the fort for their protection, Mary did not see the crowds of Osage that had gathered there in earlier years. However, the Indians who came to trade at the fort were impressed with her from the start. They admired her beauty, her colorful clothes and garden, and her book collection. Her skills at horseback riding and piano playing became legendary. Her wedding gift from her husband had been her saddle horse, which she brought to the "wilderness" to use. She came and went as she pleased, and she and George often rode miles from the fort. While men at the garrison staked bets on how long the "somewhat spoiled" Mrs. Sibley would last in the wilderness, some of the Indians began sending their children to listen to her read or play the piano. With Mary's sister Louisa living at Fountain Cottage, Mary began teaching her as well as some of the Indian girls and settlers' daughters, offering them piano lessons as well as instruction in reading and writing. Never formalized, these lessons nonetheless marked the beginning of Mary's career as an educator.

Mary did not often lack for company. She met newcomers and those neighbors who had settled in the Fort Osage area before the fort had been abandoned in 1813. Most of the white settlers who had come before the war had done so with the idea of profiting from the fort. In 1810 Risdon H. Price of St. Louis had entered into a business proposition with Dr. John Robinson to provide pork for the garrison. Robinson had come to Fort Osage as a physician in 1809 at the invitation of the fort's commander, Eli B. Clemson, but soon accepted the position as subagent. For a couple of years, Ira Cottle and his family made the Fort Osage area their home, arriving with a herd of 110 cattle in order to supply beef to the soldiers. Meanwhile, Mrs. Cottle and four Indian women began a candle-making business. In 1810, Dr. James H. Audrain built a cabin one mile east of the fort. On his 1811 trip down the Missouri, Brackenridge reported he had "stopped at the clearing of Mr. Audrain, who is opening a farm below the fort." Audrain had been justice of the peace in a township west of St. Louis, where a county still carries the Audrain name.

Once the garrison returned to Fort Osage after the War of 1812 and the region became safer, families began moving into the area. Land that had previously been unavailable to settlers was opened up following Congress's approval in 1811 of the Fort Osage treaty of 1808. These emigrants came mainly from the Southeast, leaving worn-out tobacco and cotton farms in Virginia, North Carolina, Kentucky, and the lowlands of Tennessee to claim fertile Missouri land. They were mostly Methodists, Baptists, and Presbyterians who respected education. They wanted their sons to learn how to read and write and do calculations. However, for the most part, the daughters of the settlers were expected to receive their education at home. They learned how to keep a house—how to cook, weave, and spin. They might also be taught how to read the Bible. In the eastern settlements of the Missouri Territory, subscription schools had been started before 1820. Families sent their sons to school for a fee and took turns housing the schoolmaster. An itinerant teacher or a clergyman who wanted to augment his salary held classes for three or four months during the winter when the boys were not needed to do farmwork. Fort Osage area residents did not organize a school until sometime in the 1820s when Kentucky immigrant William Buckner built a log house and opened a school southwest of Fort Osage.

In 1816, when schooling was not available, Mary Sibley became concerned about the lack of education for the pioneer children, especially the girls. She also worried about the Indian children. Although she hoped the Osage could keep their unique culture, she realized that to get along in their changing world, they would need to learn to speak and write English. George agreed with her, but he also agreed with Big Soldier, a venerable Osage chief who had visited Washington twice and had received medals of friendship from the government. Big Soldier told Sibley that he admired the white men with their fine houses and farm equipment, but he did not like their "chains" of civilization. He admonished, "You, yourselves, are slaves, slaves to the lives you lead." He did not want to adopt the white man's ways. "Talk to my sons," said Big Soldier, "perhaps they may be persuaded to adopt your fashions, or at least to recommend them to their sons; but for myself, I was born free, was raised free, and wish to die free." George reported Big Soldier's speech in an 1820 letter to superintendent of Indian affairs Thomas McKenney, adding, "I was vain to combat this good man's opinion with an argument." Mary, who had never considered herself a slave to anyone or anything, was probably too young to appreciate the truth in Big Soldier's words. She respected the Osage culture but took it upon herself to teach English to any children who came to her.

George Sibley's relationship with the Indians and the trust that had developed between them also aided in their acceptance of Mary. George quickly realized, however, that the factory was not going to be as successful as it had been earlier and was concerned about his future. After having told his brother in August 1815 that he would remain in Indian service for only a short while before opening his own trading business in St. Louis, George had reversed his position by July 26, 1816. He wrote Samuel:

> At present the mercantile business is quite overdone in this country, and I presume all over the western country. There is at this time such swarms of merchants in St. Louis and the neighboring towns that store rooms are very difficult to be had. Individual sales, I am told, are barely sufficient upon an average to defray current expenses. Of course, this being the case I am deterred from embarking in the tape and bobbin business. I am convinced that I had better continue a year or two longer dealing with the Osage Indians for beaver and fur skins on account of the United States.

Sibley continued to draw the same salary from the U.S. government for his position as a factor, but since he was not as busy conducting trade with the Indians, he was happy to assume two new roles. In 1816, he became postmaster of Fort Osage. Weekly deliveries of mail and newspapers arrived at the dock to be distributed, and the fort became a collection point for mail to go out. Then, in 1817,

Thomas McKenney asked Sibley to become the Indian subagent, a job that had not been filled since the fort reopened. Now it became George's duty and pleasure to distribute annuities to the Osage.

When the Osage came to collect their annuities or to trade at the factory, they now often brought their children so that they could spend time with Mrs. Sibley. Teaching them allowed Mary the chance to communicate with children, and she always loved playing hostess. Not long after she arrived at Fort Osage, she determined that she did not want to miss any potential visitors. Arriving river travelers were generally announced well in advance. According to a story that has been repeated several times, Mary stationed a servant at the dock twenty-four hours a day to invite anyone who arrived at Fort Osage to visit the Sibley home.

If she and George had arrived at Fort Osage early enough in the spring of 1816, Mary may have played hostess to Daniel Boone, who spent two weeks at the fort beginning on April 29, 1816. Mary did meet all of the important visitors who stopped at Fort Osage during her years there, including Native Americans, government officials, European travelers, and explorers, and hosted frequent overnight guests. One such group in 1818 included Maj. Stephen Cole, Joseph Stevens, and William Ross, who told the Sibleys about finding an unusual tomb of a British soldier. While on an exploratory trip the year before, the three men had happened on to a large, oddly shaped mound about six miles southeast of what is now Sedalia, Missouri. They assumed that the site was an Indian burial mound and entered it by enlarging a hole that had apparently been scratched by wolves. They found themselves in an eight-foot-square room with sod walls and a log ceiling high enough to accommodate a standing man. On a log bench opposite them was the frightening sight of a seated British officer in full military dress; he appeared alive except for the fact that his skin was leathery and his color ghostly. In return for their fascinating but eerie tale, Mary Sibley offered the gentlemen an excellent meal, a jig or two on her piano, and a comfortable place to sleep.

In the fall of 1818, a different group of visitors arrived. When Kansa Indians began setting up lodges around Fort Osage, George Sibley became somewhat concerned. He learned that they had come to bargain with him knowing that he, as Indian subagent, represented the Great White Father in Washington. Sibley reported to territorial governor William Clark that the Kansa tribal leaders had told him that their former hunting grounds were being threatened by white settlers and they would like payment for this land. The good relationship the Kansa had with both Clark and Sibley had prompted them to seek some kind of agreement. After receiving instructions from Clark, Sibley sat down to three days of negotiations with the Kansa leaders. The area they were interested in selling was a parcel northeast of the Missouri River between the Nodaway and Platte rivers. In the preliminary agreement Sibley negotiated with the Kansa, the U.S. government was to pay the tribe $1,000 annually for twenty years, redeemable in merchandise, a great bargain for the U.S. government. Both current-day Independence and Kansas City developed on land ceded by the Kansa in this agreement.

The Osage had also signed a new treaty with the U.S. government during the summer of 1818. They ceded more land in what is now Arkansas and Oklahoma and agreed to stay in their traditional homeland on the Osage River at Marais des Cygnes. With few Indians in the area and more settlers arriving, the usefulness of Fort Osage came more and more into question.

First, the Office of Indian Affairs decided that the garrison at the fort was unnecessary. George Sibley thought otherwise. He did not believe the military should leave until the surrounding settlements had grown strong enough to defend themselves. Sibley reminded William Clark that the troops were stationed at the fort not only to protect settlers but also to protect the Indians from settlers invading their land and attacking them and to restrain the various Indian nations from fighting among themselves. By July 1819, however, Sibley realized his arguments were useless. He wrote his brother that it was just a matter of time before the Fort Osage garrison left. Meanwhile, he expected five or six hundred soldiers to pass through Fort Osage on their way to three new posts being established on the upper Missouri: one at Council Bluff at a place the Indians called "Omaha"; one near the Mandan villages; and one at the mouth of the Yellowstone River. At the same time, a scientific expedition was to ascend the Missouri via steamboat.

During the early summer of 1819 reports arrived at Fort Osage that the Sixth Infantry Regiment had passed St. Louis and was waiting at Fort Bellefontaine for the scientific part of the expedition to arrive in the *Western Engineer*. A group of two hundred soldiers had already passed Fort Osage by barge in the fall of 1818 and had encamped a few miles north of the mouth of the Kansas River. Only a few fortunate soldiers would travel with the scientists on the steam-powered *Western Engineer,* while others embarked on three small steamboats, the *Jefferson,* the *Franklin,* and the *Johnson.* The *Jefferson* sank near Franklin, Missouri.

The *Western Engineer* was the first steamboat to navigate the Missouri River beyond Franklin. Secretary of War John C. Calhoun had commissioned the *Engineer* for an official expedition to explore the Missouri and its tributaries. The leader of the expedition, Maj. Stephen H. Long, had asked that the boat be designed to resemble a sea monster, hoping to frighten the hostile Indians he expected to encounter on his journey. Built by the American Inland Navy and launched on May 29 near Pittsburgh, Pennsylvania, *Western Engineer* was already a legend by the time it reached Fort Osage.

After passing through St. Louis and St. Charles to much acclaim, the *Engineer* had stopped in Franklin to load up on mulberry wood, which supposedly generated the boat's fastest speed of three miles an hour. As the steamboat approached Fort Osage, its smoke could be seen a full six miles away. For two hours, Mary and George Sibley, along with the Indians, settlers, and army personnel on hand, waited at the docks to witness the *Engineer's* arrival. They heard their first steamboat whistle, and then they saw the creation. According to an observer:

> The bow of this vessel exhibits the form of a huge serpent, black and scaly, rising out of the water from under the boat, his head as high as the deck, darted forward, his mouth open, vomiting smoke, and apparently carrying the boat on his back. From under the boat at its stern issues a stream of foaming water, dashing violently along.

Among the passengers was Titian Peale, a painter and naturalist, who later became director of the Philadelphia Museum. As Capt. John O'Fallon wrote George Sibley, on the bow was mounted "an elegant flag painted by Mr. Peale, representing a white man and an Indian shaking hands, the calumet of peace and a sword."

Edwin James, who wrote an account of Major Long's Yellowstone Expedition, recounted that when the *Western Engineer* left Fort Osage after a ten-day visit, it had as passengers for the first ten miles "Mr.

Sibley and his lady, to whom the gentlemen of the party were indebted for numerous hospitable attentions during their stay at Fort Osage." In fact, it had become customary for Major and Mrs. Sibley to accompany their guests a short way by boat and then return to the fort by horseback.

The voyage of the *Western Engineer* represented a milestone in several ways. The frontier now extended beyond Fort Osage. The fort's own garrison had left, although military officers continued to travel through Fort Osage on their way to new outposts. When scurvy and other illnesses set in at the Council Bluff camp during the winter of 1819-1820, many officers took refuge with the Sibleys. George Sibley's commonplace book, in which he recorded board bills, shows numerous military officers staying at the fort during the following two years. In one instance, Lieutenants Pentland and Shay arrived at Fort Osage on February 9, 1821, and stayed until after breakfast on February 14, when they set off for Council Bluff. On February 27, Lieutenant Pentland returned, having lost his way. The last boarders recorded were in April 1822.

Although the garrison was removed, Sibley continued to operate the factory at Fort Osage and in 1821 opened a subfactory, run by Paul Baillio, near the Great Osage village. Only a year later, however, the U.S. government called for the complete closure of Fort Osage and the factory system. Sibley had foreseen that the end of the trading house system was inevitable, as he had confessed to his brother. Nonetheless, he had continued to buy goods for the factories and to act as though he would stay at Fort Osage and operate the trading houses indefinitely. Perhaps several changes that came to Missouri Territory in 1821 had caused George to believe that the fort-factory system would continue.

CHAPTER 5

Fort Osage Closes

The year 1821 was an auspicious one in Missouri history as well as in the lives of Mary and George Sibley. In that year, Missouri became a state; the U.S. government opened a subfactory near the Big Osage village; the first trade expedition to Santa Fe departed, and Harmony Mission was established near the Marais des Cygnes in present-day Bates County.

During Rufus Easton's term as a delegate for Missouri Territory in the U.S. Congress from September 17, 1814, to August 5, 1816, he had proposed that Missouri be considered for statehood as a free state, a recommendation Mary strongly supported. Nothing came of his proposal. When Easton ran for reelection as a territorial delegate in 1816, he lost to proslavery candidate John Scott in a campaign largely focused on the issues of Spanish land grants and the sale of public lands. Thinking the election results were inaccurate and hoping to reclaim his position, Easton protested the vote. The results of the election were overturned, causing Scott, a hot-tempered former Virginian, to challenge Easton to a duel. Perhaps remembering his friend Gideon Granger's advice from years before, Easton replied to Scott, "I don't want to kill you, and if you were to kill me, I would die as a fool dieth." In the follow-up election Scott won.

The question of Missouri statehood did not come up again until 1819 when Congress reviewed Missouri Territory's application. Representative Scott wanted Missouri to enter the union as a slave state, and a major conflict developed over the slavery issue. In 1819 there were eleven free states and eleven slave states, leaving the U.S. Senate evenly divided with twenty-two senators from each section. In the House of Representatives, however, the balance tipped toward the

North because of the greater population in the northern free states. Admitting Missouri as a slave state would change the balance in the Senate to favor the South and diminish the power of the northern majority in the House. The representatives from the North were unhappy with this prospect but agreed to admit Missouri as a slave state with certain restrictions. Importing slaves into Missouri would become illegal, and all children of Missouri slaves would be set free at age twenty-five. Although this legislative amendment passed in the House, the Senate rejected it. Southern politicians were angered by the restrictions, and North Carolina senator Nathaniel Macon argued for continuing to add slave states, "Why depart from the good old way, which has kept us in quiet, peace, and harmony?" On the other hand, many northern senators opposed any expansion of slavery. As Sen. Rufus King of New York stated, "The existence of slavery impairs the industry and the power of a nation." The dispute continued, and Missouri did not become a state for another two years, an indication of the great divide that existed between the North and the South over slavery.

Rufus Easton's biographer, Bruce Campbell Adamson, believed Easton was antislavery during the years 1816–1820 but then changed his opinion. Certainly, Easton, a New Englander, as well as his daughter and many other Missourians of his time, had mixed feelings about the institution. For some Missourians, the slave issue was one of constitutional rights rather than a moral issue. If other states had the right to determine whether to be slave or free, then so should Missouri. For other Missourians, slavery was an economic issue. Missouri's slave population had grown from 3011 in 1810 to 10,222 by 1820, and slave owners—at that time in the majority—had considerable slave "property" to fight for.

According to the *St. Louis Enquirer* of May 10, 1820, "not a single confessed restrictionist" was elected to the Missouri constitutional convention of 1820 called to consider the issue. J. B. C. Lucas of St. Louis confirmed that he had been a candidate for the convention but was not chosen after he stated that "it would be proper to limit the importation of slaves to five years or a short period." Lucas said that he was "called an emancipator and this is the worst name that can be given in the state of Missouri."

Easton, although not in favor of immediate emancipation, agreed with his former colleague that slavery should be limited and then stopped. He had been critical of the old French clique in St. Louis whose members were longtime slave owners, even though he had slaves himself, as did Mary and George Sibley. Perry McCandless has observed that in view of the opinions expressed during the struggle for Missouri statehood, "Missourians appear to have convinced themselves that the abolition of slavery in the state was against the welfare of the slaves" themselves. Easton's ambivalence undoubtedly mirrored the feelings of many others in Missouri—though, as McCandless noted, no one asked the slaves.

A solution to the issue of Missouri statehood became possible in 1820 when a part of Massachusetts applied to become the state of Maine. Henry Clay, a representative from Kentucky, proposed the Missouri Compromise, thereby becoming a hero to many, including Rufus Easton, who named his last-born son after Clay. The provisions of the compromise were: (1) Missouri would be admitted to the Union as a slave state, (2) Maine would join as a free state, and (3) slavery would thenceforth be prohibited north of the 36° 30' line of latitude, which was Missouri's southern border. Although the basic disagreements between the North and the South remained and Missourians continued to struggle with the issue, Missouri was admitted to the Union on August 10, 1821, as a slave state, maintaining the balance of free and slave states.

Missouri's admission to the Union resulted in a new role for Mary's father. Rufus Easton had never ceased being active in politics while pursuing his law practice and real estate investing, and Mary continued to offer him advice, solicited or not. In 1821 Missouri's first governor, Alexander McNair, appointed Easton attorney general, a position he held until 1826. Chosen over eight other towns that had vied for the honor, St. Charles became the temporary capital of Missouri while a new "city of Jefferson" was being built. This was convenient for the Eastons, who had moved to St. Charles in 1817 or 1818 and lived at 201 South Main Street, on the southwest corner of Main and Madison, where they had built a large, two-story brick house, with an office on the main floor and their private residence on the second. Before his appointment as attorney general, Easton had become "a leading lawyer of St. Charles and enjoyed a marvelous practice at the Bar," according to St. Charles historian Edna McElhiney Olson.

As attorney general, one of the first issues Easton dealt with related to slavery. While realizing that Missouri had been admitted to the

After Missouri gained statehood in 1821, the first state capitol was established in St. Charles, where George Sibley had bought property. Mary Sibley's father, Rufus Easton, was appointed attorney general for the new state and served until 1826. He continued to live in St. Charles. (Missouri Department of Natural Resources, courtesy State Historical Society of Missouri, Columbia)

union as a slave state, he nevertheless could not see perpetuating the institution. He proposed an amendment to the Missouri Constitution of 1820 that would reverse the clause that granted the Missouri General Assembly the ability to pass laws to prevent free blacks and "mulattoes" from settling in the state. The General Assembly agreed to the amendment, although Easton's success was short-lived. Judge J. B. C. Lucas and Edward Bates, who had studied law under Easton, convinced the General Assembly in 1824 to pass an act that would force former slaves to "sue for their freedom." In other words, free blacks could settle in Missouri only with the court's permission.

While Rufus Easton was involved in the new state government, Abial took care of their still growing family. Two of Mary's sisters had left home by 1821. Joanna, who was two years younger than Mary, was married in the Eastons' St. Charles house in 1818 to a Dr. Quarles. Louisa, who had spent parts of 1816 and 1817 with Mary at Fort Osage, was sixteen in 1821 when she married Archibald Gamble, again at the St. Charles home. Shortly after the Gambles' wedding,

Abial Easton took the rest of the children, except for fourteen-year-old Alton, who was at boarding school, to Fort Osage for a visit. Sibley reported to his father-in-law in a letter of September 10, 1821, that "Mrs. Easton and the children are in good health," including thirteen-year-old Russella, nine-year-old Joseph, seven-year-old Langdon (who apparently had injured his head but "has healed up perfectly"), three-year-old Alby, and baby Sarah, who would be one in October. Another daughter, Medora, was born in 1823, and another son, Henry Clay, followed in 1826, completing the Easton family of seven girls and four boys.

The location of the new state capital at St. Charles was a happy coincidence for the Sibleys as well as for the Eastons. Although the town was only twenty-five miles closer to Fort Osage than St. Louis, it was more convenient to reach from the west. George Sibley's government work sometimes took him to the capital city, providing an excuse to visit Mary's family, to whom he had become close. Perhaps the Sibleys were already considering relocating to St. Charles, although it is not obvious from letters exchanged between George and his father-in-law. Apparently both men were experiencing financial woes, but especially Easton, presumably caused by his Alton investments. Sibley wrote to Easton in September 1821: "You continue to remind me in almost every one of your letters that you want money and that such and such sums are absolutely necessary to save certain property, etc. I am fully aware of all your embarrassment as regards your pecuniary affairs, and can only repeat to you my regrets that I have not the power to offer you any assistance." Sibley was busy opening a new factory in the heart of Osage country, and his expenses for trade goods would soon be the source of his own financial problems.

Since the treaty they had made with William Clark in 1818, the Osage tribes had given up another parcel of land to the U.S. government and had agreed to reside in their homeland at the confluence of the Marmiton and the Marais des Cygnes rivers. The Fort Osage factory was seventy-eight miles north of the Big Osage village, and the Osage wanted a trading post and blacksmith closer to their village. They appealed to Gov. William Clark, who approved sending a delegation to Washington to talk to the Great White Father. On July 20, 1820, the secretary of war wrote Clark that the Osage "complaints are not without sufficient reason. The factory [at Fort Osage] and blacksmith's shop are certainly very inconveniently located for them; and I have, accordingly, informed them, that the latter would be removed to their village." Thomas L. McKenney, superintendent of Indian trade, agreed. He thought that a subfactory of Fort Osage near the Osage village would strengthen control over the tribe and further the interests of the government trading system. Paul Baillio, who had been a subfactor at Chickasaw Bluffs near Memphis, was to be factor of this trading shop, but during the summer of 1821 he lay sick in Franklin, Missouri. Therefore, George Sibley, as Baillio's supervisor, saw to the building and stocking of the new Osage store, which functioned as part of the Fort Osage factory.

Besides needing a trading store, the Osage wanted a mission school and a mill. Visiting their southern neighbors near Fort Gibson in what is now Oklahoma, they had learned that missionaries at Union Mission were teaching the "arts of civilization" to the Arkansas tribes. Upset at what they saw as favoritism, the 1820 delegation of Osage had appealed to President Monroe for a school. Monroe and Col. Thomas McKenney had been impressed and thought that much good might be accomplished by establishing a school among the Osage along the Marais des Cygnes. Colonel McKenney wrote the American Missionary Society in New York: "I have had this moment a most interesting interview with the Chief Councellor and principal warriors of the Osages of the Missouri. The object of their deputation is to solicit the introduction of the school system among their people, and to pray for the means of civilization. I wish I might send you the chief's talk; but to do so I should have to paint as well as write. He is a most eloquent and able man." The idea was approved by the secretary of war, who granted "The Great Osage Mission" the authority to teach "the Indians the common elements of education and the ordinary mechanic and domestic arts."

On March 3, 1821, a mission group embarked from New York City to the land of the Osage. The United Foreign Missionary Society of New York had received over one hundred applications from missionaries to take on this work, but finally ten adult males, fifteen adult females, and sixteen children were selected. Most of the men were college graduates and descendants of Revolutionary War heroes. Nathan P. Dodge was chosen as superintendent to direct the establishment of the mission, which was to be called Harmony. It was funded by churches, which had donated ten thousand dollars, and by the U.S.

government, which had provided a one-thousand-dollar donation plus nine hundred dollars per year to support the mission school.

The journey to the land of the Osage was harrowing from beginning to end. The missionaries kept a daily record, reporting that after leaving New York they traveled to Philadelphia aboard the steamboat *Atlanta* and then by wagon to Pittsburgh. On April 19, 1821, they boarded two keelboats to take them into Missouri Territory. Ten days out on the Ohio River, Brother and Sister Newton's daughter was born, but a week later the baby died, followed by Sister Newton. A boatman fell overboard and drowned in the Ohio. On May 9 the missionaries reached the Mississippi River and knew they still had "between six and seven hundred miles up stream which will be laborious indeed." On June 5 they reached St. Louis, where they met with Governor Clark and "the elder and younger Chouteaus, who gave us instructions concerning the Osages." Following this briefing, the missionaries had another six weeks of travail on the Missouri River, where they fought sandbars and a boatmen's strike (the first recorded strike in Missouri). When they finally reached the mouth of the Little Osage, they were overwhelmed by the sight of "the most beautiful prairie." Shortly thereafter, the missionaries passed Auguste Pierre Chouteau's trading post and arrived at the Osage village, where they were warmly welcomed.

"The Indians appear very friendly," Otis Sprague wrote from the site of Harmony Mission. Mrs. Jones recorded that she and five of her white brethren were invited into a wigwam, and one of the Indian women could speak enough English to tell them that they had "great confidence" in the missionaries. "They say our hearts appear good outside now, but they wish to try us three years, and in that time they can judge whether they are good inside." The Osage women gave the missionaries gifts of watermelon and corn and seemed "fond of our children." They would "often clasp them in their arms and bring them presents of nuts." The chiefs assured the party that they would protect them from injury. The missionaries were grateful for the Indians' kindness after their hard journey. Amasa Jones remarked that the Osage were "in appearance as noble a race of people as I have ever seen. . . . The men are large and well built—not many of them are less than six feet in height." To the missionaries the Osage seemed willing and anxious to be "both civilized and Christianized."

In addition to being impressed with the friendliness of the Osage,

HARMONY MISSION FOR THE OSAGES-1821-BATES COUNTY

Harmony Mission was established at the request of the Osage, who wanted both a school and a factory near their homeland. (Missouri State Capitol Mural by William Knox, courtesy State Historical Society of Missouri, Columbia)

the missionaries were overwhelmed with the beauty of the country and the resources it provided. On August 25, they finished unpacking their boats and setting up tents about two miles north of the confluence of the Marmiton and the Marais des Cygnes rivers, near the town of Papinsville, named for Melicourt Papin, a fur trader from St. Louis who had settled there in 1809. Apparently both Mary and George Sibley were on hand to help the missionaries unload and identify the location George had recommended for their site, which was convenient to the trading post and to the Osage village. Sprague wrote his brother: "Our buildings will be erected on the river bank, but sufficiently remote to give us a spacious and handsome green in front. In the rear we have a vast prairie, covered with grass, yielding in the uncultivated state, from one and a half to two tons of hay on the acre. On either side of us we have good timber in great plenty. We have, also, near at hand, an excellent spring of water, stone coal, limestone, and clay of the first quality for making bricks." Sprague also reported that the Indians "frequently visit us; and we feel the assurance, that some of their children will be sent to us as soon as we are able to accommodate them."

The school did not open as planned. Fever and ague struck on August 27, keeping the missionaries from getting started. Half of the autumn of 1821 passed, and they still had no "huts" or shelter of any kind. Building finally began only due to the arrival of three benevolent strangers passing through en route from Arkansas to St. Louis. "Directed by an unseen hand," as missionary Amasa Jones wrote, the travelers volunteered their services for a week to attend to the sick and get building materials in order. Then help arrived from Union Mission, so that cabins were available for the surviving missionaries to weather the rough winter. Mrs. Montgomery and her newborn, Mrs. Belcher's infant, and Mr. Seeley had all died. By Christmas, the remainder of the missionaries had recovered.

To begin with, Harmony Mission got all its provisions through the Osage factory. The first winter, which arrived early, was cold and harsh. On December 7, Rev. Nathan Dodge and Samuel Newton set out through the snow along the seventy-eight-mile missionary trace from Harmony to Fort Osage to stock up for the season. They wanted to buy cattle, hogs, potatoes, seed-corn, and cornmeal, among other items. Mary and George Sibley put them up at Fountain Cottage, "where we were treated with much attention and kindness," according to Dodge. The missionaries held a public worship service at the Sibleys' home on December 16 before returning to Harmony with their provisions. After some discussion, George Sibley persuaded them not to take potatoes back to Harmony, predicting they would freeze and rot and assuring the men that he would deliver potatoes to them in the spring. Sibley's diary later noted that on March 24, 1822, the promised "perfectly sound" potatoes were taken to the missionaries.

Another connection between the mission and Fort Osage involved the use of the factory and subfactory interpreter, William S. Williams, more generally known as "Old Bill." Williams began teaching the missionaries the rudiments of the Osage language; with his help, they put together an Osage dictionary and notes on the most important parts of grammar and sentence structure. Old Bill even helped the missionaries translate some chapters of the Bible into the Osage tongue. However, Williams's close association with the missionaries did not last as long as it might have, because a rift developed over the story of Jonah and the whale. Against Williams's advice, the missionaries had used the Jonah story in a Sunday service for the Osage. At the end of the preaching, one of the Osage chiefs rose and said, "We have heard several of the white people talk and lie; we know they will lie, but that is the biggest lie we ever heard." This incident and the missionaries' frequent cries for help from Old Bill at their convenience rather than his finally led to the day when Williams "laid aside his Christianity and took up his rifle and came to the mountains."

Although the missionaries had lost their interpreter, they had not lost their prime advocate, Mary Sibley. As soon as Mary learned that Harmony Mission was in the planning stage, she was eager for the mission to establish a school. She had been teaching English to Indian children who came to her, but their visits were sporadic, and she could not hope to have the effect that a full-fledged school might have. With a school at the heart of Osage country, the children would no longer have to travel the seventy-eight-mile trail to Fort Osage. In January 1822, the mission school began with three pupils of mixed descent: Catherine Stearnes, Kansa and Osage; Catherine Strong, white and Osage; and Sarah Cochran, French and Osage. By the end of the month, according to the mission report written by Reverend Pixley, there were "twelve children from the natives, of both sexes, and of all sizes; five of the full-blooded, and seven halfbreed." Pixley also noted: "These children are certainly as interesting and active as the generality of children among the whites, and I have sometimes thought they are more so." The missionary teachers marveled at the talent of their students, not realizing that some had started their education with Mrs. Sibley. The twelve-year-old daughter of an Osage chief knew all her letters and was writing well after only six days in school, an accomplishment the teachers thought quite remarkable.

One other exceptional student was the daughter of Sans Oreilles, the Osage warrior who had guided George Sibley to Salt Mountain. This child's arrival was heralded in the *Journal of the Great Osage Mission*. On June 17, 1822, factor Lilburn W. Boggs "arrived from Fort Osage, bringing a package of letters and papers. . . . He brought up Mrs. Sibley's little girl to attend our School." Mary Sibley had been custodian of Sans Oreilles's daughter since his death, a tribute to the relationship she had developed with the natives. She wanted to have the girl in the mission school, and Dr. Belcher wrote to George

Sibley: "Sans Ora's [sic] daughter which Mrs. Sibley was anxious to purchase or have under us, we with the assistance of Mrs. Boggs, have procured and she is now in our school bearing the name of Mary E. Sibley to be altered at your suggestion. . . . The girl is hereafter to look to Mrs. Sibley for a mother." A provision in the charter of Harmony Mission was that "any Society or Individual who shall contribute $12 annually for four years for the Education of a Heathen Child, shall have the privilege of giving that child a name." Since Mary Sibley had provided the funds to educate Sans Oreilles's daughter, the child became known as Mary Sibley at the mission. Young Mary became a fairly accomplished student during her one-year stay at Harmony Mission. When her blood mother came to get her, missionary Nathan Dodge recorded his regret, saying Mary departed "probably to spend her life in heathen slavery."

Three other children joined the school at the same time as Sans Oreilles's daughter, two of them grandchildren of Sans Oreilles. According to Dr. Belcher, their father had shot another man in front of George Sibley's door and had then been forced to leave his wife and village. Thus, Dr. Belcher added, "Poverty has brought them to us. One a girl, the other a boy . . . I have been particular knowing your affection for the Ora [sic] family."

Other students of note included children brought to the school by Sans Nerf and Moneypushee, both of whom had been part of the Osage delegation that visited Washington during the summer of 1820. The two boys enrolled by Sans Nerf were his daughter's sons by Cheveux Blancs the Younger, the grandchildren of Cheveux Blancs, the venerable Big Osage chief. Also enrolled in the school, according to Kate Gregg's account in the missionary records, were two of Bill Williams's daughters. Harmony Mission's 1828 educational report described the accomplishments of both Rebecca and Mary Williams. Rebecca Williams, who is listed on the Harmony roll for 1824-1825 as Pawnee, French, and Osage, may have had the name Williams only because Old Bill brought her to the school. She would stay at the mission for six years and acquire the art of spinning cotton as well as literary skills. Mary, who was listed as half English and half Osage, was, according to Nathan Dodge, "a fine promising girl—Was in the school near four years and became an excellent scholar & is now living in the family of her Uncle who is a white man." The missionaries were grateful to have at least one of Bill Williams's blood daughters as a student, as Mary spoke English, which was especially helpful given the Lancastrian educational methodology used.

The Lancastrian Monitorial school system, developed by Joseph Lancaster in 1806, was designed to allow a single schoolteacher to lecture a large number of students while older students, called monitors, provided crowd control and taught the younger students. The original purpose of the system was to provide inexpensive public education. It enabled the missionaries, who were still striving to master the Osage tongue, to use their bilingual students to teach those students who had not yet learned English. Although the Lancastrian method proved a failure in public schools, it was useful for teaching the Osage children. As Pixley noted, "The Lancastrian method of instruction is peculiarly calculated to interest them." Mary Sibley would use the Lancastrian technique some years later when she taught Sunday classes to German immigrants in St. Charles.

Although Harmony Mission could claim success with certain students, the missionaries themselves recognized that the educational outcome was not what they had anticipated. Students who were enrolled for an extended time learned to speak English, acquired domestic skills, assumed Western-style dress, and practiced the Christian religion. Perhaps learning about white ways was success enough. However, the missionaries did not reach many children, and the school never grew very large. According to the mission journal, Cheveux Blancs the Younger blamed the lack of attendance on "meddling traders," whom he saw as a "great hinderance [sic]" to the school as they "contrive every plan and adopt every kind of artifice and intrigue to lead or drive the Indians away from the trading houses established by the government, in order to gain the trade for themselves." Most detrimental to the school's success were the treaties of 1822 and 1825, which ended the trading house system and moved the Osage away from their homeland. Nonetheless, in 1824 there were twenty-four students at Harmony; in 1825, thirty-eight; in 1826, twenty-four; in 1830, forty. Then the enrollment dwindled until the school was closed in March 1836.

Reflecting on the Harmony Mission School in 1834, long after she had left the Fort Osage area, Mary Sibley had mixed feelings about what the school had accomplished. Although she admired the missionaries and their techniques, she also hoped that the native culture of the Osage could survive. In her journal, Mary wrote: "I do hope that the efforts of the Missionaries may be successful to preserve the remnants of at least some of those powerful tribes who once inhabited this vast Country. There is not hope from any other source. If they become Christianized they will adopt the habits of civilized life and thus provide for themselves the means of subsistence." However, being able to support themselves and becoming "civilized" might negate the native cultures completely. This dilemma could not be resolved.

When the mission at Harmony was abandoned, many of the missionaries stayed on. Some continued to serve as ministers in nearby communities. Others became farmers. Writing to his brethren in Worcester, Massachusetts, Amasa Jones admitted to missing his friends but did not plan to move back east. He hoped to convince them to move to "a land of plenty . . . surrounded with all the comforts of life which we need or should desire except your society." Understanding the love the Osage had for their homeland, Jones said, "We have too long resided in this mild climate to endure the long and cold winters of the north. Again we have too long lived in a country surpassing almost all others in fertility to be again satisfied with the rocky and sterile regions which gave us birth." Mary and George Sibley felt the same way about the area, which George Sibley said was called "The Garden of Missouri" for "good reason." They would need to determine if they would stay in the area if and when Fort Osage closed.

Harmony Mission School was purposely located near the subfactory that George Sibley and Paul Baillio had opened the summer before to serve the Big Osage. However, the trading house system was doomed. George Sibley had fought persistently to keep the government trading houses going and had supported Thomas L. McKenney, superintendent of Indian affairs, in his efforts, providing him with information about the success of the factories in terms of both trade and political control over the Indians. Other Missourians, however, including Sen. Thomas Hart Benton and powerful traders such as John Jacob Astor, spoke against the factories, saying they denied independent traders their rights under the free enterprise system. The law abolishing trading houses passed in March 1822.

CHAPTER 6

Pioneers on the Western Frontier

In August 1822, U.S. Indian agent Richard Graham arrived in Fort Osage to officially close the fort and trading post. He called together the Osage chiefs. For $2,329.40 worth of merchandise, they signed a new treaty, which took away the benefits they had received in the treaty of 1808, including the guarantee of a factory. At the same time, George Sibley and subagents Paul Baillio and Lilburn Boggs relinquished their jobs. Sibley agreed to buy the rest of the Fort Osage trade goods, since neither Baillio nor Boggs had any capital. The purchase left the Sibleys with a debt they would need more than ten years to repay.

George could not look to his father-in-law for financial aid, and apparently his own father did not or could not help either. In a letter he wrote in anticipation of a visit to Fort Osage, Dr. John Sibley informed his son that his nephew Cyrus Sibley was worth $60,000 to $100,000 from his mercantile business in Mobile Bay, information that evidently did not help George. John Sibley, who had been appointed by President Jefferson in 1804 as the Indian agent in Natchitoches, had been dismissed in 1814. Since then he had contributed articles to various newspapers and ventured into politics, becoming a Louisiana senator. He had not yet met Mary, but in his October 29, 1821, letter, John said he looked forward to seeing his daughter-in-law. He also passed along the news that "the work begun by Mr. [Moses] Austin who has died has been taken up by his son." John Sibley was knowledgeable about the Red River Indian tribes and Spanish Texas, and he predicted that close to fifty thousand Americans would immigrate to Texas. He also anticipated that there would be a convention to write a constitution and that "I will probably be appointed commissioner to fix our western boundary," thereby giving him the excuse to travel west to Fort Osage. Perhaps John Sibley did visit George and Mary in 1821 or 1822, but no record of such a visit has been found.

About the time the missionaries had arrived to establish Harmony Mission, the Sibleys had witnessed the beginning of a lucrative trade with Santa Fe, then still part of Mexico, which gained its independence from Spain in 1821. In September 1821, on the first Santa Fe expedition, William Becknell of Howard County and three associates had stopped at Fort Osage with $300 worth of goods packed on their horses that they intended to trade for horses and mules. When Becknell returned with favorable reports about the profits he had made, three other groups began making plans for expeditions the following spring. Becknell himself, on his second trading trip, took the first wagons into Santa Fe, going south through the site of present-day Dodge City and then approaching Santa Fe from the east through San Miguel. On his return from this expedition, Becknell wrote: "An excellent road may be made from Fort Osage to Santa Fe. Few places would require much labor to make them passable, and a road might be laid out as not to run more than thirty miles over the mountains."

Becknell is rightfully credited with the opening of the Santa Fe Trail, but he was not the first to conceive the idea of a trading route from Fort Osage to Santa Fe. On January 18, 1809, a few months after the opening of Fort Osage, George Sibley wrote his brother that if Great Britain and the United States went to war and if Spain should enter, "it is likely this [Fort Osage] will be a rallying post from whence to attack Santa Fe; we could march there and Seize their rich mines in less than 20 days. And I have no doubt if we have a war, but seize them we shall." Sibley knew there were lucrative trading possibilities in Santa Fe. He had firsthand accounts of the city from Dr. John Robinson, who had traveled with Zebulon Pike on his 1806 expedition. Sibley became well acquainted with Robinson during their two years together at Fort Bellefontaine; they grew even closer when Dr. Robinson served as deputy Indian agent at Fort Osage and the men shared dinner conversations.

Col. Benjamin Cooper of Howard County also made an early trading trip to Santa Fe. In April 1822 he and his two nephews, Stephen and Braxton, and twelve or thirteen other men went through Fort

Osage on their way West. When they arrived in Santa Fe, Colonel Cooper approached the governor of the city, who told him, "Go back to your men and tell them we are glad to see them." Enthusiastic reports of that expedition led to speculation about the riches to be had in Santa Fe. George Sibley became very interested. By the time the Cooper party returned, not only did George know that Fort Osage was going to be shut down, but he had already agreed to sign for the $7,000 that he, Boggs, and Baillio would owe the government for Indian goods. He was anxious to find a money-making opportunity. Nonetheless, he and Mary decided not to get involved in Santa Fe trade but rather to stay at Fort Osage and expand their farming operation.

Between 1822 and 1825, the Sibleys devoted themselves to their farm at Fountain Cottage. George continued to look for government work, hoping for a way to repay his debts. He depended on Rufus Easton, who was still attorney general for the state, to keep him up-to-date on Missouri politics. Mary, too, stayed in close contact with her family, visiting as frequently as possible, given her obligations at the farm. She always had been a second mother to the siblings who were close to her in age, especially Louisa, whom she had helped rear. Now she advised them frequently, if not in person then by letter. In 1823 she seemed particularly concerned about her brother Alton. At age fifteen and a half, he was not the student she thought he should be. She exhorted him to study hard so that he would be qualified to enter military school: "You are liable to be sent home if you do not by proper exertion induce your tutors to believe you are worthy to remain a pupil." In her January 23 letter Mary reminded Alton:

> Remember that in this country the advantages of rank and fortune are not required to make the hero or statesman. But more independently and more gloriously you rise in the estimation of the world solely by your talents and merit. Let this idea my dear Alton stimulate you to depend on your own exertions to establish yourself an honorable character.

Apparently Mary's concerns were not without basis, for although Alton was admitted to West Point in 1824, he dropped out in 1827. After studying medicine briefly, he gave up that pursuit before finally settling into a respectable military career.

After Fort Osage was shut down in August 1822, it was not long before new settlers began tearing apart the blockhouses and barracks that had so recently been a part of the Sibleys' lives. By the following summer, the hewn timbers of the fort had all been taken to use in houses, leaving the site of the fort bare. Many of these new homes were being built illegally in the so-called Garden of Missouri area, an allotment that was still reserved for the Kansa Indians. This very fertile forty-mile-wide strip of land stretched from Fort Osage west to the mouth of the Kansas River and south beyond the Missouri border. In an 1824 letter, Sibley wrote government officials that the Indians were no longer using this allotment and that over one hundred squatters had already settled there. He urged the government to "extinguish" Indian title to the Garden of Missouri and purchase this "valuable part of the country from the Kansas to whom it is useless, for a trifling sum, and sell it to your own citizens who desire and will make valuable use of it, for an immense profit." Sibley suggested that $1,000 in merchandise would be a "fair price."

Visitors continued to pass through Fort Osage, even after it closed. Some Indian tribes, who still considered George "The Little White Father," came to consult him. One famous traveler, Duke Paul of Wuerttemberg, arrived in 1823. George received a letter introducing the duke from Wilson P. Hunt, a former trader for John Jacob Astor who later became the second husband of Nancy Anne Lucas. Now a prominent businessman in St. Louis, Hunt wrote: "Please show all the kindness you can to Paul, Prince of Wirtemburgh [sic], who leaves here for the Missouri on a scientific voyage. He is passionately fond of the study of natural history." Mary showed Duke Paul her customary hospitality, while George advised him on his scientific explorations.

Fort Osage was on the route traders took to Santa Fe, so the Sibleys heard about many of these trips, both the good and the bad experiences. On their second trek to Santa Fe, the Coopers were accompanied by thirty to thirty-five men, including Joel P. Walker of Fort Osage. This expedition, as Kate Gregg described it, was "unique for its hair-raising episodes." Indians stampeded the travelers' horses, leaving them with only six mounts. They nearly starved, ran low on water, and got lost, among other troubles. The Coopers' experience inspired one of the first cries for assistance from the government to provide safe passage for travelers.

Sen. Thomas Hart Benton was a strong supporter of westward expansion and encouraged the development of the Santa Fe Trail. (State Historical Society of Missouri, Columbia)

The idea of a road to Santa Fe began to receive attention from the U.S. Congress in 1824. Not only had trade to Santa Fe increased but so had Indian attacks. With the closing of the Indian factories in 1822, the U.S. government lost control over Indian trade as well as leverage to affect Indian behavior. What native tribes had formerly bought at the government trading houses, they could now buy, or seize, from traders on the open trail. They could then make their escape on horseback and not fear having their trading rights cut off. Stories published in the *Missouri Intelligencer* in Franklin reported attacks by hostile Indians necessitated Congress taking speedy action to protect the traders en route to and from Santa Fe.

Missouri senator Thomas Hart Benton carefully organized and orchestrated the campaign for support for the Santa Fe Trail. Many letters, with remarkably similar Benton-esque language, were sent from all areas of Missouri, and petitions were forwarded to Missouri congressmen. The governor of the state, Alexander McNair, wrote the federal secretary of state on April 27, 1824, listing six reasons that the trail should be laid. Benton made these very same six points in his presentation to the Senate, relying on information he had received from Augustus Storrs, who would soon become U.S. counsel for Santa Fe.

Storrs had been a part of the eighty-three-man Le Grand expedition, which had started ten miles south of Fort Osage and then followed the missionary trace. Alexander Le Grand was elected captain of this expedition about three days from Franklin. With twenty-three vehicles and 156 horses, the traders ventured on across the "vast plain which lies between the Mississippi and the Rio del Norte," according to Thomas Hart Benton, who published Storrs's account of the trip as a government document. "But romantic as it might seem," Benton proclaimed, "the reality had already exceeded the visions of the wildest imagination. . . . The fruit of these enterprises for the present year amounted to $190,000 in gold and silver bullion and coin, and precious furs; a sum considerable in itself in the commerce of an infant State, but chiefly deserving a statesman's notice as an earnest of what might be expected from a regulated and protected trade." Benton went on to claim that cotton was the principal article of exchange, "which has the peculiar advantage of making the circuit of the Union . . . which grows in the South; is manufactured in the North; and exported from the West." Thus, Benton promoted a regulated trail from the edge of the frontier, presumably Fort Osage, to Santa Fe as a money-maker for the United States.

After almost a year of promoting his cause and educating his colleagues, Senator Benton presented a bill on January 3, 1825, authorizing the president to cause a road to be built between Missouri and the boundary of Mexico. The bill went to the Committee on Indian Affairs before being taken to the Senate on January 25, where Benton reiterated his six points: (1) cotton was a national trade commodity; (2) a controlled road would prevent future Indian atrocities; (3) the route was without major obstructions and would be easy to construct; (4) missionary possibilities existed; (5) there were precedents to build roads between the United States and areas controlled by another nation; and (6) regulated trade with Mexico would be very lucrative for the United States.

After listening to Senator Benton's presentation, Congress passed the bill. On March 3, President James Monroe signed the law authorizing $10,000 for surveying and marking a road to the Mexican settlement of Santa Fe, the "Highway between Nations," as Benton called the trail. In addition, Congress provided $20,000 "for treating with the Indians for the right of way." When all was said and done, it was uncertain whether the amount of potential trade and the dangers of traveling to and from Santa Fe necessitated the trail or whether Sen. Thomas Hart Benton's ambition was responsible for it.

In any case, only thirteen days after the Santa Fe Trail bill had been signed, a new president, John Quincy Adams, appointed three commissioners to mark out the trail: Benjamin S. Reeves, Pierre Menard, and George C. Sibley. Reeves's selection was expected. He was considered one of the most influential men in Missouri and certainly in Howard County, which had become the center of the Santa Fe trade. Reeves had been active in Missouri politics since his arrival in 1819, serving on the Missouri Constitutional Convention, as state auditor, as state senator, and most recently as lieutenant governor, a position he resigned in order to accept his appointment to the Santa Fe commission. The choice of Pierre Menard, a merchant, trader, and partner in the St. Louis Fur Company, also seemed logical. Menard resided in Kaskaskia, near St. Louis, and was active in the St. Louis fur trade. However, Menard declined his appointment for personal reasons and was replaced by Thomas Mather. Mather, an Indian agent, younger than Menard, also had many advantageous business connections. While neither Reeves's nor Mather's appointment surprised anyone, George Sibley's commission astounded many, no one more than Sibley himself.

Sibley learned of his appointment on April 12, 1825. He was riding toward St. Louis, where he was going to ask Richard Graham, a U.S. Indian agent, to delay collection on the payment owed to the government for the factory supplies that he had committed to purchase. He was hoping to avert the disaster of having to start all over at age forty-three. Since he had secured his debt with property, he knew that all the land he had purchased was in jeopardy and he could lose everything, including 640 acres on Wild Horse Creek, 800 acres on Plattin Creek near Herculaneum, 200 acres near St. Charles, two lots in St. Louis, 640 acres on Sny Ebore Creek in Lafayette County, and 320 acres in Jackson County.

The uncertainty of his situation had caused him great anxiety for three years, while he tried unsuccessfully to earn a living as a farmer. During that time his debt had increased to nearly $9,000. Sibley must have been so engrossed in his thoughts that he barely noticed a familiar rider coming toward him as he neared Arrow Rock. Thomas J. Boggs had set out from Franklin, where he had heard about the appointments of the commissioners, to find Sibley and get his endorsement to be the secretary for the Santa Fe commission. Sibley, taken off guard, declined to make a commitment to Boggs; he still wasn't convinced that the president had actually selected him for such an important position.

George Sibley's selection as Santa Fe commissioner should not have been a shock to him. He had demonstrated his loyalty as a government employee, working for seventeen years as a factor. One of the commissioners needed to have writing and reportorial skills, and Sibley's literary ability was known to Presidents Jefferson, Madison, and Monroe, to whom he had submitted reports on Indian affairs. He had also written articles for the Franklin newspaper and others. Moreover, Sibley had established a long association and good rapport with the Osage and Kansa tribes with whom the commissioners would have to negotiate for safe passage along the trail. Because the Osage had recently signed a new treaty that was not favorable to them, they would likely consider further agreements only with someone they knew and trusted.

The Osage treaty of 1825 gave the Little and Big Osage the "protection of the Government so much desired by them" in return for their lands in the state of Missouri and the territory of Arkansas. Although the Osage treaty provided for two thousand dollars upon signing, four thousand dollars in merchandise, and seven thousand dollars annually for twenty years, many believed that the benefits did not justify the fact that the Osage were forced to leave the land that had been promised to them forever. William Clark, who presented this treaty to the Osage, admitted that the agreement was the hardest one he had ever had to sign. He worried that it might even cause him to be barred from Heaven, as he considered it almost sacrilegious to deny the Osage their homeland at Marais des Cygnes. Nonetheless, the treaty was signed, and many believed it would take someone like the Little White Father, George Sibley, to deal further with the Indians.

For many, however, Sibley's qualifications were not sufficient for the job. During the fall after his appointment, critics called him a "public defaulter" and maintained that there were others far more deserving and qualified than Sibley. Although he had many friends who came to his defense, Sibley himself demonstrated in the years that followed that he deserved the commission and earned the title of "Mr. Santa Fe" that Kate Gregg claimed for him.

On April 25, 1825, Sibley arrived in St. Louis and received the official commission from Washington, D.C. He also had in hand a letter from Sen. Thomas Hart Benton suggesting that he keep a journal to note geographic details of the trail, which might become a published government document. At once, Sibley accepted his commission and vowed to both the president and Senator Benton to carry out the purpose of the congressional act. After receiving relief from paying his debt until the survey was completed, Sibley immediately began organizing the commissioners, requesting that they meet in St. Louis at their earliest convenience. Reeves and Sibley met on May 10, a week after Sibley had hoped to start back to Fort Osage.

The commissioners' first tasks involved finding qualified people for the expedition and setting a timetable. The $30,000 allotted by Congress drew wide attention, attracting some two hundred applicants for the positions of surveyor and secretary. Reeves and Sibley selected Joseph C. Brown as surveyor and Archibald Gamble as secretary. These appointments, which proved to be excellent choices, immediately drew criticism, as Brown and Gamble were members of the same church and had worked together on previous surveys. In addition, Gamble was George Sibley's brother-in-law, having married Mary's sister Louisa in 1821.

Besides making these and other appointments, the commissioners decided to start the survey in mid-June from Fort Osage. However, the expedition did not leave St. Louis until the end of June. "The detention here so much longer than I expected when I left home is not a little hurtful to my private business," George wrote on May 1; "I shall probably not see my home for two months to come . . . & as I left my affairs as a man merely going away for two weeks my farm and stock must necessarily suffer very much in my absence." Mary had gone to St. Charles to be with her family, and on June 25, George left St. Louis for St. Charles, where he took leave of his wife, her family, and friends.

Finally, on July 17, 1825, the Santa Fe expedition "set out from its camp near Ft. Osage and proceeded with the work," according to Sibley's diary. Benjamin Reeves and Thomas Mather had joined Sibley on July 11 while the rest of the party shod horses, repaired wagons, and made final preparations for an expedition that Sibley rightly expected would be "fraught with difficulties & privations & hazards innumerable." The group left a few days ahead of Sibley, who stayed at Fountain Cottage until July 29 to nurse his bilious symptoms and to catch up on farmwork and correspondence, which included writing to ask for an additional appropriation of $12,000 for the survey. Mary and George Sibley could not have guessed that he would not return home until October 1826, more than a year later, though George did have some misgivings that he might never come home at all. He left Fountain Cottage sadly, expressing how much he would miss his "dear wife." During the next year, Sibley's letters and journal indicate that Mary and George's separation was a hardship for both.

The survey party, traveling in the heat of the summer, suffered greatly. Greenflies were so bothersome that the group tried to travel at night, making collection of data difficult. On August 8, camped at a beautiful grove of trees on the Neosho River, the commissioners greeted the arrival of fifty chiefs and warriors of the Osage tribe who had been brought there to negotiate by Archibald Gamble. Sibley suggested "the propriety of naming the place 'Council Grove' which was agreed to, & directed Capt. Cooper to select a suitable tree, & to record this name in strong and durable characters—which was done." With the aid of interpreter William S. "Old Bill" Williams, the Osage decided to allow the commissioners to mark the road through their land and permit free usage of it forever in exchange for $300 worth of goods given immediately and $500 more in goods to be on order with A. P. Chouteau, Pierre Chouteau's son, who had graduated fourth in his class at West Point and now had several trading posts in the Arkansas Territory. The Osage departed expressing their entire satisfaction, except for a few individuals who did not like the way their chiefs had distributed the goods on hand.

Sibley entrusted one of the Osage, Belle Oiseau, with a letter to Mary Sibley and one to Lilburn Boggs, Sibley's trade partner. As the party continued on its mission, the Santa Fe commissioners experienced equal success talking with the Kansa Indians. Old Bill had been sent out from the survey group to invite the chiefs and warriors to meet at a convenient place east of the Arkansas River. On August 17, the Kansa representatives signed a treaty with the same provisions as the one signed by the Osage.

Having negotiated safe passage from the Indian tribes and completed a preliminary survey of the trail to the Mexican border by September 11, the survey party awaited instruction from Washington about continuing the survey through Mexican territory. When word still had not come by September 20, Reeves, Sibley, and Mather were of differing opinions as to what to do. They did not want to get caught in the mountains in the winter. Finally, Sibley proposed that one of the commissioners along with the surveyor, interpreter, nine men, and two wagons should go on to Santa Fe. Reeves and Mather agreed to having Sibley travel ahead while they returned to Missouri. They would then meet Sibley in Santa Fe on July 1 of the next summer to complete the survey. Sibley spent the winter in Santa Fe, becoming friendly with the governor of the Mexican state of Nuevo México, Antonio Narbona, while awaiting permission from the Mexican government to continue the survey.

Sibley had two objectives in Santa Fe. His reports to Washington and his public correspondence demonstrate his resolve to carry out a complete and accurate survey of the Santa Fe Trail. He also took the opportunity to investigate trade opportunities and ways to profit from that trade. Although the judgments against Sibley's holdings had been suspended while he was working on the survey, he would need cash when he returned to Missouri in order to keep his properties. Sibley's letters to Mary and his diary reveal his concern about money and his health, worsened by anxieties about their future. He wrote, "A principal reason for my entering upon this duty is the hope & belief that it may be beneficial to my health, which tho' not exactly *bad* at this time, is & has been for 3 or 4 years indifferent." The winter in Santa Fe did prove beneficial to Sibley's health. When in Taos on March 26, 1826, he wrote: "A fine day. Since my Return from S'ta Fe, I have got entirely well again, and am now in as good health as I ever was."

George Sibley had left Santa Fe in February with the intention of sending part of the survey party home to save expenses. He himself stayed in Taos, where in May 1826, he received permission from the Mexican government to survey the western part of the trail. Sibley awaited commissioners Mather and Reeves. He waited all of June, all of July, and twenty-four days of August before he departed without them to conduct the survey of the trail from Taos, arriving safely back in Missouri in October.

Mary Sibley had not stayed at Fountain Cottage during all of George's long absence. She spent time in St. Charles with her parents and may have even conducted informal classes for her sisters and neighboring girls. Mary was certainly at Fountain Cottage to greet George on his return. She also had been there when a party of Missouri Indians passed by Fort Osage on their way to meet with William Clark in St. Louis, as Clark indicated in a thank-you note he sent Mrs. Sibley on August 4, 1826: "I had the honor of receiving your letter of the 9th of June by a party of Missouri Indians who pass by your house on their way to this place. The friendly part which you took, in procuring or becoming responsible for a Canoe for those Indians to the Missouri deserves all the grateful feelings which Indians possess, & for which I beg you to accept of my thanks."

Sibley's sojourn at Fountain Cottage was not a long one, for the survey was still not complete. Mounds needed to be marked on a corrected survey from Fort Osage to the Mexican boundary. When the commissioners met in St. Louis on January 20, 1827, they voted to entrust Sibley with correcting the final survey, settling the accounts, and sending in the report. Sibley accepted this responsibility, demonstrating once again his dedication to the job.

He left Fort Osage in May 1827 to complete the survey. Two months on the trail with unbearable heat, pesky mosquitoes, and persistent flies did not deter Sibley, although he narrowly escaped death as he returned home. During a thunderstorm, his tent was struck by lightning. "The shock awoke me to the most painful & alarming Sensations," George wrote in his diary, "for my Right Side which I lay on was for a Minute bereft of feeling nearly, My foot Seemed Reduced to jelly, having no feeling. A whirring noise passed thro' my ears continually, & the tent was filled with Smoke and Strewed with Splinters." George's compass was "Reduced entirely useless so that I am obliged to Stop the Survey here." Two days later, on July 8, George returned to Fountain Cottage and reunited with Mary.

The Sibleys now had to face their financial obligations. George had been promised eight dollars a day for the survey, but he had yet to be paid. Before the resurvey, Sibley had offered the government "all I have, except an unconfirmed claim to the tract on which I live in Jackson county." Apparently, the government determined to take all of the Sibleys' land, including the Jackson County property. Fountain Cottage farm was put on the auction block in 1827; it was purchased by Archibald Gamble, Mary's brother-in-law. Ten years later, Judge Gamble laid out the town that would become known as Sibley. In the meantime, Mary and George prepared to move.

George Sibley and Thomas Mather met in October 1827 at Eckart's Tavern in St. Charles, Missouri, to submit a final report on the Santa Fe Trail. All three commissioners signed the report and forwarded it to Washington on October 21. After the report was lost, Reeves and Sibley sent a duplicate copy on December 7, along with "two packages of maps, field books, &c.&c." This set of reports was also lost. Exasperated beyond even his seemingly unlimited patience, George Sibley made still another report in triplicate, had it signed, and hand-delivered it to Washington, where he was asked to appear to answer questions about the "over-run" of $1,504.54. Sibley could hardly be blamed for referring, at one point during the questioning, to the Highway between Nations as "Benton's d——d Santa Fe road." It would be seven years before Sibley and the other commissioners would receive payment for their work.

After two years spent surveying the Santa Fe Trail, describing the country and the rivers, drawing pictures of the landscape, suffering through delays, criticism, and hardships, George Sibley was ready to stay in one place. Mary had taken care of the Fort Osage property, worked with Indian children, and lived on her own. She, too, was prepared for a more settled life. They had to move, since their land had been sold, and they chose St. Charles, which was once again a sleepy river town. In 1826, the capital had been removed to a new city named after President Jefferson, and Rufus Easton had returned to his legal practice. The Sibleys found a house down the street from Mary's parents, at 230 North Main, and prepared to leave Fountain Cottage.

CHAPTER 7

The Great Awakening

When the Sibleys left Fort Osage, Mary was twenty-eight years old and George forty-six. They were childless and seemed likely to remain so. They had few assets except the worldly goods they packed for the trip to St. Charles. They loaded Mary's piano, furniture, and books on a boat and traveled in reverse the river journey they had made in 1815. After the earlier journey, Mary had written her father she had not seen a white man; now viable towns existed at Lexington, Franklin, Boonville, Jefferson City, and Washington, and other settlements and farms were visible along the way.

St. Charles, where Mary and George planned to make their new home, was one of the oldest towns west of the Mississippi River. It had been founded in 1769 by Louis Blanchette, a French Canadian fur trader who did not realize that the territory had already been transferred to Spain. He called the area Les Petites Cotes, "The Little Hills," which described its topography. In 1791 the Catholic residents of Les Petites Cotes dedicated the first church to San Carlos Borromeo, and the town became known as San Carlos del Misuri. The Spanish named Blanchette the commandant of the District of San Carlos in 1791 and granted land to the community to be used as "common fields." By 1796, when Auguste Chouteau surveyed San Carlos, the town had begun to grow as Anglo-Americans crossed the Mississippi into Spanish Territory. Eighty families lived in or near San Carlos, including Daniel Boone and his family, by the time of the formal transfer of Upper Louisiana from Spain to France to the United States in 1804. Following the transfer, the name of the village was anglicized to Saint Charles. It was here that Lewis and Clark had their last taste of "civilization" before leaving on their expedition. By

When George and Mary Sibley moved to St. Charles, they lived for a time in this house at 230 N. Main Street, which had been built in 1817. According to the St. Charles Historical Society, they moved to Linden Wood in 1831. (Wolferman photo)

1819, St. Charles had grown, according to the census list, to include 981 whites, 124 slaves, and 5 free Negro residents. It served as the state capital from 1821 to 1826, but when state officials left for Jefferson City it returned to being a small Missouri River town.

The St. Charles that Mary and George saw when they arrived on May 16, 1828, probably looked little different from the city of today. While the Arch now dominates the riverfront area of St. Louis where the Chouteaus and other French families once lived, the old town of St. Charles, listed on the National Register of Historic Places, retains most of its original character. The Easton house at 201 South Main still stands along the brick street that runs close to the riverfront, as does the house Mary and George moved into at 230 North Main. A short walk enabled Mary to see her father every day, a practice she kept up for the rest of his life. She remained her father's most devoted child, and their relationship was one of mutual respect. Mary often played her piano and/or sang for him, and they discussed current events and politics.

While George tried to put the finishing touches on the Santa Fe survey, find a new career, and settle his financial problems, Mary began teaching a few students. She also spent time with her siblings who still resided at home. In 1828 Alby was ten; Sarah, eight; Medora, five; and Henry Clay, two. Abial Easton encouraged Mary to take a hand in educating the last of her brood. Mary's two closest sisters, Joanna and Louisa, were married, and Alton was in the army. Russella was nineteen and either at home or at finishing school. Brothers Joseph, sixteen, and Langdon, fourteen, were at boarding school.

Although the U.S. government would not compensate George for his years of work on the Santa Fe Trail until 1834, he had paid off most of his trade goods debt by handing over to the U.S. government the land he had accumulated for speculation. In March 1828 he received a note of acknowledgment from Josiah S. Johnston, attorney and U.S. senator from the state of Louisiana, who happened to be married to George's half sister, Ann Elizabeth Sibley: "The Secretary of the Treasury has determined to accept your proposition by taking your lands at the prices fixed in your letter. They will be sold by the Marshall [sic] and the district attorney will bid the price fixed."

Johnston added that Sibley would be given time to pay the balance of his debt in cash, thanks to the help of his father-in-law's friend and former law partner "Mr. [Edward] Bates," who "has been very useful in this arrangement." Thus, the U.S. Treasury, in exchange for the land Sibley offered, paid all his trade good debts except for $829.81, which he still owed to the St. Louis merchants Tracy and Wahrendorff. Sibley had originally hoped to keep his tract of land near Fort Osage, but when that land was sold, perhaps he decided instead to keep a tract he had bought on speculation near St. Charles. In any case, shortly after the Sibleys arrived in St. Charles, they decided to start a farm on land they owned outside the city limits. Because of a magnificent grove of linden trees on the site, they named it Linden Wood.

How the Sibleys acquired this acreage is puzzling. According to *History of St. Charles County*, George Sibley learned in 1829 that "120 acres adjoining St. Charles" had defaulted to him. The reason given was that Sibley had backed an army friend, acting as his bondsman in the amount of $20,000. When the friend could not pay his debts, the only asset available to repay Sibley was the 120-acre lot on which Linden Wood College would eventually be built. Although this is possible, evidence of a default is scanty. Neither the original survey of the plot nor the first property deed gives any indication that the Sibleys acquired their St. Charles property through default.

The Missouri Historical Society in St. Louis has on file the 1792 survey for the land. According to Survey No. 185, written in French, Louis Blanchette leased this acreage, which was part of the Prairie Haute Common Fields, to his two cousins. When Blanchette died in 1793, the property became part of his estate, was appraised at 3,500 piastres, and was sold to two buyers. The earliest deed on the Linden Wood property on file with the office of the St. Charles County Recorder of Deeds is dated August 4, 1829, and is signed by Mary and George Sibley. According to this document the Sibleys owned three parcels of land: "two hundred and eighty arpens [the old French unit of land roughly equivalent to an acre] situate[d] on the upper Prairie so called near the Town of St. Charles . . . purchased by said Sibley at different periods from T. F. Reddick & wife, M. I. Devor & wife, and Thomas P. Capes & wife, as appears of Record, in the recorders office at St. Charles." Thus, the Sibleys by 1829 had pieced together three pieces of land, totaling 280 acres, which included the 120 acres on which they started Linden Wood.

Shortly after arriving in St. Charles, Mary and George went out to inspect their property. The grounds were so tangled and overgrown that they would have to "clear away enough thickets in order to obtain a view of the land and its situation," George recorded in his notes. To obtain funds to build a house and clear the land, the Sibleys decided to mortgage two tracts of their property, valued at $550. Borrowing $523 from Edward Bates and Thomas Biddle, they listed their assets:

1 Negro woman slave Betty—35 years
1 Negro man slave Edward—Betty's son—17 years
1 Negro man slave George—Betty's son—15 years
1 plain cherry side board
1 dining table, cherry
1 cherry breakfast table
1 wagon work table
1 mahogany side board
1 mahogany secretary and bureau
1 cherry bureau
1 pine clothes press

1 paper case
1 Seth Thomas clock, ornamented with Masonry emblems
1 cherry high post bedstead with cornice
1 field bedstead of sugar tree (maple)
3 feather beds
1 hair mattress
bed clothes
12 common green chairs
10 yellow Windsor chairs
1 yellow settee
2 domestic carpets
1 dozen: silver tablespoons, dessert spoons, teaspoons
6 silver numbers
1 silver sugar tongue
1 set blue china ware
1 set penciled French china ware
1 set Brittania ware
2 dozen glass tumblers and wine glasses
6 decanters
1 candle shade
1 pair plated candlesticks.

Mortgaging these possessions allowed them to get on with their lives.

In his journal George wrote: "Early in the summer of 1829, [we] employed Arch Johnson of Boone to clear twenty acres of Linden Wood at $6.00 per acre." As soon as Johnson finished this job, George noted that part of the cleared land was set aside as a garden, which "was planted with corn, potatoes, pumpkin and squash—firm crops." George's detailed journal entries indicate how proud he and Mary were of their St. Charles property.

By the end of July 1829, still not having received payment for the Santa Fe survey, George and Mary took out another mortgage on their St. Charles property. In the August 4, 1829, mortgage deed, the Sibleys acknowledged their $829.81 debt to Tracy and Wahrendorff of St. Louis and their two prior mortgages to Bates and Biddle. Using as collateral the 280 acres they themselves had purchased, the Sibleys said they fully intended to pay off their debts by August 4, 1830. Meanwhile, they mortgaged not only their property but other worldly goods, including:

one negro man slave named Edmund, aged 23 years—one other negro man slave named Henry, aged about 23 years, one other negro man slave named Baltimore, aged about 17 years, one other negro man slave named Edward aged about 17 years—one other slave named George aged about 15 years, and one negro woman slave named Betty aged about 36 years. Also the following list—one stallion called Rodrick, ten brood mares and their foals. Fifteen 1 and 2 year old colts, Three mules, Fifty-six asses, one other stallion, one Roan Gelding, ten oxen, Seven milk cows, twelve young cattle, one waggon, one ox cart. Five plows with chains.

George Sibley stated in the deed that he was "now opening a farm and making improvements."

In August 1829, with part of the land cleared and a garden planted, the Sibleys started construction of their log home, but progress was slow. "The cold weather has played mischief with our preparation for moving," George noted in his journal, as Mary anxiously anticipated having a place to call home. Although the Sibleys were able to get their livestock—over one hundred head of horses, mules, and cattle—transported from Fort Osage in November, Mary feared, "It will be Christmas before we get out to Linden Wood." On December 23, 1829, they "moved out to Linden Wood having so far completed the cabin and outhouses as to winter comfortably." By the spring of 1830, the Sibleys were settled. George noted that, despite the early cold weather, "the winter was mild and the stock got through very well." With her vegetable garden planted, white curtains at the windows of her new house, and geraniums set, Mary truly felt she was at home.

According to *History of St. Charles County,* on the very first day they had visited their property, "the Major and his wife . . . stood on the brow of the hill overlooking the town and a widespread and beautiful landscape," including the Missouri River, and "resolved that upon this spot they would lay the foundation of a school for young ladies." Mary had recognized her affinity for teaching, but it is unlikely that she and George moved to St. Charles for the purpose of opening a school or that the tangled prairie they acquired inspired them to do so. Mary Sibley's journal, which she did not start until 1832, indicated that the idea of the school evolved through her success with tutoring students in her home and teaching Sunday school. Also, despite George's recent hardships as Santa Fe commissioner, he maintained his steadfast devotion to government service. He had not decided to forsake his area of expertise to open a girls' academy and would, in fact, hold other government jobs.

St. Charles historian Edna McElhiney Olson added to the Linden Wood lore by writing, "Mary Sibley at once began to open a school, as she loved to teach, and saw a great need for a school here. A log cabin was built near the edge of this property that could accommodate 20 boarders. For many years the Major and Mary lived in the wing of the log cabin so she could be near the students." The beginning of what would become an excellent college for women was a bit exaggerated in the retelling. Mary did not begin a school at once, and the log cabin in which the boarding school began was simply the Sibleys' home, which was added on to as needed over the years; it was not originally built to accommodate twenty students.

However, Mary did see a need for a school for women. In 1818, Mother Philippine Duchesne had opened a Catholic school in a drafty log cabin in St. Charles, which came to be known as the first free school west of the Mississippi River. Because she only had two students, she had moved the school to Florissant, but in 1828 she returned to St. Charles to establish the Academy of the Sacred Heart. Even though most education for girls occurred in the home, Mary thought that a non-Catholic girls' school was needed. She "perceived that young American ladies would have to be well educated to take their places in the growing West, as leaders of home and social life," as her obituary in a June 1878 St. Louis newspaper was to note.

Establishing a date for the opening of Mary Sibley's girls' college is difficult. Did the school start when she began tutoring children in her parents' home in 1826 or in her own home or when she took in the first boarders or when an actual school building was constructed? Linden Wood's centennial historian, Dr. Lucinda de Leftwich Templin, dated the founding of the college to 1827, the date the university uses today. However, this date was based on the misreading of a letter to George Sibley from Dr. Belcher about the Harmony Mission School, which Templin assumed concerned Mary Sibley's school. The letter was dated 1824, which she mistook as 1827. In any case, since George was still finishing the Santa Fe Trail survey in 1827, and the Sibleys did not move their belongings from Fountain Cottage until May 6, 1828, according to George's diary, it is not possible that the Sibleys founded Linden Wood in 1827.

Mary's school doubtless started just the way her informal Fort Osage school had begun, by teaching her sisters. In the fall of 1830, Mary's twelve-year-old sister Alby came to Linden Wood to study. Mary's first two paying students arrived in 1831. Early in 1832, before Mary actually began to make plans to expand the Linden Wood cabin to provide room for more students and create a real boarding school for women, she experienced what she called a "spiritual awakening."

Mary wrote about her newfound religion in her spiritual journal, begun at the same time as her "awakening." She noted that "it is known to most of my dear friends that I have been for a long time deeply interested in an investigation of the claims of the Bible to be the word of God." Although there is no reason to question Mary's zeal or her awakening, her experience was definitely part of a nationwide movement. A period of increasing evangelism started in the 1790s and became widespread in the 1830s. Called the Second Great Awakening and led by ministers such as Charles Grandison Finney, who became pastor of the Free Presbyterian Church in New York in 1832, the movement from the onset took on several causes besides religion. Inspired by the ideal of the Declaration of Independence that all men are created equal, the Second Great Awakening led the way for crusades for temperance, suffrage, and the abolition of slavery.

Mary wrote in her spiritual journal that her "dearly beloved friend" Margaret Lindsay also inspired her religious conversion. Margaret was buried on March 15, 1832. Mary had stayed with her friend the entire week before she died, except for a few hours one evening when she attended a meeting at Margaret's request. Margaret's goodness, patience, and endurance of pain as well as her faith impressed Mary. Margaret's funeral, attended by "old and young, black and white . . . a very large concourse of people" including three clergymen, encouraged Mary's conversion. Despite protests from her mother, she decided to join the Presbyterian church to which Margaret "had belonged ever since it was organized and I may add was an ornament of it to the hour of her death."

Abial Easton, whom Mary knew to be averse to those who chose to make religion their profession, surprised Mary with her emphatic opposition to her daughter's religious calling. Abial rejected all sects of religion, but she held a "stronger and more peculiar aversion to the Presbyterian Church." In fact, her mother had told a friend, Mary recorded, "that she would rather have followed her children to the grave than to see them become Presbyterians." Mary had hoped that her sister Alby could join the church at the same time she did, but Abial adamantly refused her consent.

On March 25, 1832, prior to becoming a church member, Mary decided to visit Abial, "knowing that my mother was offended with me for the step I had taken." When Mary arrived at her "father's house," she found that all her family had left for church to witness Mary's confirmation except her mother. Mary tried to assure Abial "with tears" that she had "no intention of offending her," but Abial rushed out of the room only to return a few minutes later to vent "her feelings in a torrent of abuse upon the Presbyterian Church and its agents, said that by joining them I had abandoned her, and she gave me up & would have nothing more to do with me." Mary was "very hurt" by her mother's tirade; she wrote in her journal that she had "always reverenced and loved my Mother more than any human being." Nonetheless, Mary felt duty-bound to receive the ordinance, be baptized, and become a Presbyterian. Her mother's opposition merely made her more determined and provided her with proof of the "Savior's words: 'Think not that I am come to send peace on earth, but a sword. For I am come to set a man at variance against his Father, & the daughter against her Mother.'"

Despite her mother's disdain of her new religion, Mary did not give up trying to get Abial to attend church or at least to make the commitment necessary to enter heaven. Although Mary had little luck, Abial did not totally disown her daughter, as she had threatened. In fact, during the next month of April 1832, Mary and her mother were so preoccupied with preparations for Mary's sister Russella's wedding to St. Charles lawyer Thomas Lilbourne Anderson that Mary neglected not only her journal but also her efforts to convert her mother.

However, Mary refused to accept that her mother would not accept a savior. Apparently, Mary did not see the irony when she wrote in her journal: "The more certain we are that we are right the more intolerant do we naturally become, when we apply the rule to others which we have laid down for ourselves." On June 22, 1832, Mary confided in her little book that her "dear friend, Elisa Baker, agreed to unite to day in praying for the conversion of my Dear Mother."

Even with her friend's help, Mary did not succeed in convincing her mother, who was apparently as stubborn as her daughter. When, in September, Abial became ill, Mary was alarmed. She felt it her "duty to talk to her and urge upon her the necessity of seeking a Redeemer." On the other hand, Mary worried that speaking to her mother about religion would agitate her so much that "I should do more harm than good." When Abial began to recover, Mary herself developed a fever and a sore throat and was in considerable pain. After being confined to her bed for ten or twelve days and missing a much anticipated trip to St. Louis, Mary regretted her inability to be patient. When she felt better, she wrote in her journal that "God afflicts his children for their good," although she did not repent of her continued efforts to save her mother.

During 1832, the year of Mary's "awakening," she also began to teach Sunday school. On April 21, just a month after she joined the church, she took it upon herself to find a schoolroom, "the little log cabin near Mr. Cole's place," and to notify children of the Sabbath school she planned to open the very next day. Although she complained that there were so few children at her country school on some Sundays that she would have been better off going to hear a sermon herself, Mary deemed it her "duty as teacher to be at my post." By July 1 of that same summer, Mary found her Sunday school full, mostly of "Dutch" children, as the Germans were known. A significant number of Germans had immigrated to the St. Charles area in the 1830s, partly due to the publication in Germany of Gottfried Duden's optimistic observations about opportunities for settlers in Missouri.

These German children, Mary observed, "appear very anxious to learn." Although she "had to lecture them upon the propriety of keeping silence during the time of prayer—and to do it through an interpreter, a little boy, the only one among them who can speak English," Mary felt that they comprehended. She showed the children pictures from the big Bible, which had many etchings in it, and brought along fruits that were described in the Bible to teach their names. More important, she felt that God understood both the children's language and hers. Mary must have found the experience of conducting these Sunday school classes for immigrant children very similar to teaching Indian children at Fort Osage; by using one child as an interpreter or "monitor," she was utilizing the Lancastrian

Method employed by the missionaries. Sabbath school prepared Mary for the fall 1832 opening of Linden Wood.

Mary noted in her religious journal on July 5, 1832: "At the particular request of their parents I consented to board & teach about half a dozen young ladies a year." Mary's spiritual enlightenment now became a driving force. She saw the school as a place for "disseminating the truth, for as Solomon says, 'Wisdom is the principal thing; therefore get wisdom: and with all thy getting get understanding.'" Mary added, "I hold our Country will never prosper unless the people get knowledge." She was determined to establish a school that would impart religious as well as academic training.

The missionary nature of her Christianity immediately caused contention. Six students were due to start school that fall, but the parents of the two who had been boarding students in 1831, Theodosia Hunt and Ann Russell, were hesitant to allow their children to return. Theodosia was the daughter of Mary's oldest friend, Nancy Anne Lucas Hunt of St. Louis. Interestingly, in her journal, Mary refers to Theodosia as the granddaughter of Judge Lucas, her father's colleague, not as her friend's daughter. Apparently, Mrs. Hunt was hesitant to allow Theodosia to be in Mary's care now that Mary had become a Presbyterian, fearing that she might exert undue influence on Theodosia to abandon her Catholic religion, or rather, as Mary wrote in a rather lofty tone, to abandon "her obedience to the Church of her Forefathers for religion in reality neither she nor her mother know much about." Mary noted that she was not of the "disposition to take particular pains to make a convert" of Theodosia, "unless the simple assertion of what I believed truth should have that effect." She did offer Theodosia's mother the opportunity to withdraw her daughter: "When you placed her [Theodosia] under my care, I was not a professor of religion, being now I trust a follower of Him who said, 'My kingdom is not of this world.'. . . The necessary consequence is that I must be somewhat changed in my opinions, feelings and actions. I hope the change will not make me less alive to the responsibility of my charge—nor less attentive to those duties devolving upon me as a teacher." Mary continued, "If you fear the consequences, you are at perfect liberty to take her home. It will not wound my feelings for you to do so." Mary observed that although Theodosia did not possess "an investigating mind," she was "extremely amiable" and "gifted, in several excellent traits of character." Apparently, this report satisfied Nancy Anne Lucas Hunt, who decided to keep Theodosia at Linden Wood.

Ann Russell had come to Linden Wood in July 1831 as Mary's first boarding student. Ann's father, William Russell, the founder of the Missouri Pacific Railroad, had known the Easton family as well as both Mary and George from St. Louis. He also was familiar with Linden Wood's location on the outskirts of St. Charles, and he claimed in a letter written from his new home in Arkansas to George Sibley: "No other place anywhere in my knowledge would have been so entirely satisfactory to me." Russell had insisted that Mary take Ann as a student, because "her manner, her pronunciation, her walk, and some of her gestures require improvement, but I am not capable of advising how it should be done." He wanted a finishing school for his daughter where she would learn how to dance and how to read, but not attend public balls or read "amusing and entertaining novels." William Russell got more than a finishing school. When he sent Ann back for the fall 1832 session, he wrote to tell the Sibleys how impressed he was with Ann's achievements as a scholar. She had learned to spell, read, and write, as well as play the piano. Russell expressed surprise that his "diffident" child had developed such self-confidence. Her improvement, Russell remarked, "has pleased me altogether better than I had expected."

Nonetheless, Russell worried about the religious component of Linden Wood, as he stated in a second letter addressed to Mary Sibley. Although Russell wanted Ann to attend church on Sunday, he did not like the idea of night meetings or of religion taught as a subject. The revival fervor of the Second Great Awakening alarmed many, including Russell, who feared that young girls were too impressionable and that the evangelical "disease" could take hold. "I am convinced that religion is a totally unfit subject to take up the time, thoughts or mind of students at school, until the mind has matured," he added. In reply, George Sibley defended the school and remained firm about its religious stance. He also maintained that no education could be complete without a study of religion:

> One can hardly be called "well educated," who has not had a thorough knowledge of the most prominent Religious and Political Systems that govern the inhabitants of the earth. . . . A Son or Daughter of our great Republic who claims a right to a place amongst the "educated"

would feel not a little mortified to be found ignorant of the Religious belief of the Chinese, the Turks, Hindoos, &tc.

Even though the Sibleys needed to attract more students in order to make the school profitable, they refused to compromise their goals of religious as well as academic and domestic education. Apparently, their arguments convinced William Russell, who not only kept his daughter at Linden Wood but also in 1836 enrolled another young lady, Lucy Ann Lewis, who had been put in his charge "for the purpose of having her educated."

A year after her spiritual awakening, aside from not keeping her religious journal as devotedly, Mary had not lost any of her zeal for saving everyone she knew. When cholera raged through St. Charles during the summer of 1833, causing a great deal of suffering and taking many lives, Rufus Easton fell ill. Mary felt helpless. She stayed with him during one night and wrote in her journal that "altho' I believed him in danger I had not the resolution to say to him all that I ought to have said on the subject of the necessity of preparing for death. Indeed, I could not bring myself to feel how dreadful his condition must be if he died without repenting and faith." Rufus Easton survived, but Mary herself contracted cholera and almost died. "I was considered dangerously ill by my physicians and I thought myself twice near death's door," she wrote after her fever had broken. "Oh! I have reason to exclaim Bless the Lord O my soul—for his loving kindness and unbounded goodness." Her escape from death increased her dedication to serving the Lord.

Mary continued trying to convince her family and friends to take up her new religion. She was thrilled to record that her sister Russella, along with her husband Thomas L. Anderson, had converted in 1833 and joined the Presbyterian Church in Palmyra, where they had relocated. "Three of my sisters," Mary wrote in her journal, "are now members of the Presbyterian Church: Mrs. Gamble, Mrs. Geyer, and Mrs. Anderson." Russella's conversion proved especially significant to Mary, as Russella had, at age fourteen, been "secretly baptized by a Catholic priest" when she was enrolled in a convent school. "The wonderful care of our Heavenly Parent" had rescued her, according to Mary. When Russella died of consumption seven years later, in 1840, Mary was gratified that her sister had found the way before it was too late.

Although many of Mary's friends also joined the church, caught up in the evangelism fever, not all heeded the calling. Mary visited some neighbors on March 27, 1833, to try "to prevail on them to go to Church, but they Alas! seem to think this world's affairs should claim their attention almost exclusively." After this failure, Mary, feeling worthless, resorted to fasting and praying, at least for as much of the following day as she could "without neglecting my household duties." On April 19 she went to "a family who are not pious, found no opportunity of speaking directly on the subject," and so left a booklet. Mary made a practice of proselytizing. As a member of the St. Charles Female Benevolent Society, she used her calls on sick people to try to convert them before it was too late. Although Mary stated that she did not think it was wise to wait to join the church until lying at death's door, whenever friends or family members became ill, she worried and hoped they would profess their belief in the Heavenly Father.

She even preached to her Christian friends. On the evening of August 13, she and her friend Mrs. R. visited about "our own religious experience and feelings" during the cholera epidemic. Before the evening was over, Mary thought it was her Christian duty "to tell her that she made herself liable to be spoken about by the enemies of religion by her attentions to Mr. H. riding with him alone." Mary claimed that although she disliked the responsibility of having to put Mrs. R. on her guard, "she took my advice kindly and I felt satisfied that I had done my duty."

Mary's journal for the first part of 1833 is full of notes on the work she did to carry out God's will. Mary also recorded her views on church meetings and sermons. For the most part, she found the talks of the Presbyterian minister, Mr. Hall, to be sage, which is perhaps why she made a special note of a sermon she heard on September 8, 1833, by "a very ignorant Methodist preacher." Mary said that when the man first started talking she "felt disposed to mirth" because of "his sad mistakes in grammar and in the use of English words." However, on reflection, Mary determined that she liked the sermon very much and thought "notwithstanding my supposed superiority this poor ignorant man might be far more highly favored in the sight of our God than myself or any of our more learned brethren."

Mary noted that a certain minister, Mr. Douglass, often held candlelight services. "My friends are generally opposed to my attending night meetings," she wrote. "I have not thought it my duty yet to yield to their prejudices." She added, "Strange that in my days of worldly folly and gaiety they never thought of finding fault with me for attending Balls, parties, theatres, etc. at night." Mary vowed not to take "any step which would be an injury to the cause of religion," and she continued to express great anxiety about her unconverted friends and family.

Mary worked enthusiastically to increase church membership. However, it was a complete surprise to her when Betty, her own slave, decided to join the Presbyterian Church on March 28, 1833, just a little more than a year after Mary's own spiritual awakening. "Among the number who came forward & joined the Church to day was my own servant woman. Who has been with me ever since I was married." Mary said she had urged Betty to attend meetings, but Betty had been unwilling to go. Mary knew "not the state of her mind until I heard her name called among the number who had resolved to connect themselves with the Church. When I looked up and saw her come forward before the congregation in answer to her name my heart leaped with joy gratitude and thankfulness to God . . . and I burst into tears." Mary wrote that she regretted that she had neglected Betty's religious education and asked God's forgiveness for not "more strictly performing my duty."

Duty to God motivated Mary to accomplish any number of goals. From the time she joined the Presbyterian Church, she decided it was important to build a proper church building in St. Charles. George agreed. Although he did not like going to church and often found fault with what the preacher said, he would on occasion accompany Mary to Sunday services: "My husband, however on my expressing a desire that he should go with me, consented," as she wrote. After all, George had been brought up in a Presbyterian household; his mother's father had been a minister, and he had nothing against organized religion. When Mary asked him to serve on the Old Blue Presbyterian Church building committee, he agreed, even though Mary would be the one to take charge.

On April 13, 1833, she went to Mr. Hall and urged him to ascertain whether there were enough church members who would expend money for the purpose of constructing a new church. A church building had, according to Mary, been "some time in contemplation and much differences of opinion expressed about it." The next

Sunday the prospective subscribers met after services to discuss a new building. After what Mary described as "considerable jarring among them so that it appeared as if we should have to give up all hopes of succeeding in building a house for the Lord," the majority authorized the committee to build. Mary remained dubious that any results would be forthcoming. She recorded in her journal that if she should die before the church was completed, which seemed entirely possible considering how long the process had been going on, she would like to give $300 to the building fund. Of course, her bequest depended on the happenstance of a friend finding and acting on her journal entry.

While she waited for a church building, George not only stood by Mary, defending her religious beliefs; he became her true partner in her Linden Wood venture. Certainly, by 1833, Mary Sibley had established Linden Wood as a school for girls. The Sibleys had augmented their log cabin by adding dormers and wings to accommodate a growing number of boarders. Regardless of whether Linden Wood actually began in 1827, 1829, 1831, or 1832, it stood as the first female college west of the Mississippi. "I commenced this spring," Mary wrote in her spiritual journal on August 17, 1833, "the little school I had last year consisting of seven or eight young girls—on the plan I have long thought necessary for the good of the rising generation. That is that women instead of being raised helpless and dependent beings should be taught a habit of industry and usefulness."

CHAPTER 8

Aunt Mary

Convinced of the potential of educated young ladies in society, Mary approached her second year of teaching at Linden Wood in the fall of 1833 as if it had been her lifelong calling. George Sibley recognized his wife's teaching ability and her determination to make a difference for young ladies. He did his part by keeping the books, figuring the prices and costs, writing advertisements, and raising produce on the Linden Wood property. He also worked for the government on various projects and reports and wrote articles for several publications.

On July 13, 1834, Sibley, along with his fellow commissioners, Reeves and Mather, finally received payment for the Santa Fe Trail survey, and the Sibleys' financial situation became of much less concern. Although it would take them another few years to pay off their debts, George Sibley breathed a sigh of relief, writing in his diary that "the whole of this business of the Road to New Mexico is at length finally and fully settled." Now he could worry about his own political future, and Mary could devote her full attention to Linden Wood.

Officially, Mary had six students in 1832, seven in the fall of 1833, and eight in the spring of that year. In spite of losing a student or two because of religious differences, Linden Wood slowly expanded. In 1834, eleven young ladies resided there, including two girls brought to the school from Palmyra by Russella Easton Anderson. Mary's sister Alby was no longer studying under her, but Sarah Easton, fourteen, was among the students, as was another fourteen-year-old, Fanny Audrain, the daughter of James H. Audrain, who had been the Sibleys' neighbor at Fort Osage. Fanny wrote her mother that she was "well pleased with the school and situation" and that she had plenty to eat. Her parents applauded a school where their daughter was treated like family. Perhaps this is when the thirty-four-year-old Mrs. Sibley became known as Aunt Mary, a name that would stick with her throughout her years at Linden Wood.

Although the school's versatile curriculum and academic excellence would gain it renown in the West, if not nationwide, Mary's religious fervor continued to pose a problem for some prospective students. She reassured parents, and George confirmed that she was not using her time "for the purpose of converting her Pupils to a belief in the tenets of her own faith." However, Mary hoped those students who were not Presbyterians would see the light. She was especially anxious to "help" Catholic girls realize that they had been led down the wrong path. Mary's journal bears witness to her prejudice against Catholicism and Catholic education, a feeling that extended beyond her outrage over Russella's secret baptism by a Catholic priest. She wrote: "I believe firmly that the Jesuits and Romans are for the most part any thing but Christians." Hoping to help young girls see the truth as she saw it, Mary contacted a friend in Louisiana, giving an account of the school's plan and encouraging him to mention to some of his friends that they might send their daughters to Linden Wood. "I am anxious," Mary wrote in her journal, "to have it in my power to educate some of the young ladies of the South that they may carry home some of those principles of the Christian religion which are so little known to the inhabitants of the catholic districts of Louisiana . . . and be the means of doing good in the world." Although Mary may not have openly advised her students to join any particular church, her religion and her moral principles pervaded Linden Wood's curriculum.

Mary made sure that parents who enrolled their students at Linden Wood understood the course of study. After that, she expected no "intermeddling." As Mary explained in her journal:

> If on due consideration with the full knowledge of my plan the parents think proper to place their children with us I expect them to have perfect confidence in my integrity and desire in all I do, to forward the best interests of their children. I should suppose it is hardly necessary for me to say, that their studies are pursued with diligence and attended to faithfully & that some of the parents have acknowledged the improvement of their children to have given them entire satisfaction.

Mr. Ridgely, a "perfectly satisfied" parent, wrote Mary "that he entirely approved my course of education." On the other hand, the father of Martha Russell (who was not related to Ann Russell), withdrew his daughter in 1834 because of "his aversion to her becoming religious." Mary told Mr. Russell that she had taught Martha "the great truths of the Christian religion which I consider essential to salvation. He went away in a great rage," saying "it was strange children could not be sent any where to school now a days but that their religious opinions should be meddled with."

A year later when Mary learned that Martha Russell was to be wed to a Mr. L., Mary wrote her "in confidence expecting this letter will never be seen by any other individual than yourself." She told Martha that she had known Mr. L. before the death of his first wife and that she had no objection to him other than to the fact that he was a Catholic. "I firmly believe it to be your duty to confess the Lord Jesus Christ before men," Mary advised Martha. "I likewise believe . . . you could not become a Roman Catholic without renouncing the religion of the Bible and denying your Savior." On page two of her letter, Mary took up the issue of children: "I might refer you to the probability of your having children to bring up in the nurture and admonition of the Lord, and I might show you by referring to many examples, how tenacious Roman Catholic families are of their right to make their children members of that Church." Mary concluded: "Understand me! I am not requiring you to break an engagement— I am simply showing you that you are bound to secure yourself and any who may be under your control, the right to become a member of a Protestant Church." If Mary was not proselytizing her students, she was certainly giving those young, impressionable minds definite ideas about what they should believe.

Mary did not limit her role as educator to her seminary for young ladies. She continued her interest in the Sunday school for immigrant children, and during the summer of 1834 she offered a Sunday class for slave children that incorporated both religious training and the basics of reading and writing. Mary wrote in her journal that she thought it "our duty," meaning the duty of Christians, and specifically the duty of the St. Charles Female Benevolent Society, "to enlighten the minds of those poor benighted creatures of their souls Salvation." She thought slaves were "entitled" to read the Bible and that it was "the duty of every Christian head of a family to instruct his servants in the Bible itself, or else place them in the way of being instructed."

When a political paper to which her husband subscribed attacked individuals for keeping Sunday schools for slaves, Mary defended her position in her journal. "Our African School has succeeded here in some respects better than we expected," she claimed. Students were learning to read and to be instruments of God. However, some masters objected to the curriculum and required their slaves to return their books. Two girls who had been permitted to attend school suddenly had to leave because, as Mary lamented, "a man who has been opposing everything good in the Village for a long time took the trouble to make their master many misrepresentations of the school." Mary said she and other members of the Female Benevolent Society "told the poor girls to pray for their masters and be obedient and all would be well with them if they served God." They did not fight to keep the girls at school but allowed them to withdraw gracefully. Aware of Nat Turner's 1831 rebellion in Virginia, during which nearly sixty whites and more than one hundred slaves died, Mary understood the fear of some slave owners. Teaching slaves was not encouraged in Missouri even before an 1847 law made it illegal. There was talk that if Nat Turner had not been taught how to read and write, none of the trouble in Virginia would have happened. Nonetheless, Mary often wrote in her journal about the benefits she thought her African students derived from attending classes.

Mary also continued to worry about the need to "save" her mother so that she "might give herself to the Lord." She renewed her efforts when Abial Easton, on returning from a neighbor's home one evening in January 1834, was severely injured after stepping on a plank that rested on ice and being "precipitated into a drain." Although in the first "intelligence we were told she was almost dead," Mary did not find her as "materially injured" as was initially supposed. However, the shock of Abial's accident sent Mary into prayer and panic because her mother still did not have a savior. Although Abial was confined to her bed for many weeks, by February 10 Mary expressed relief that her mother was recovering slowly. However, she lamented that "so far her affliction has not softened her heart and led her to seek the hand of God." Mary left her mother books, such as *The Young Christian* by Jacob Abbot, and dedicated herself to seeing her through her affliction by praying fervently. With her mother fully recovered by spring and able to get around by herself, Mary's attention shifted back to saving others.

Mary also turned to her journal to make note of the dark day, July 5, 1834, when she was called "to witness the death of my father." Although Rufus Easton had weathered the cholera epidemic of 1833, he succumbed to the disease when it struck St. Charles again the next year. Mary expressed some comfort in the fact that her father had made his peace with God before he died: "His life was for many years one of misery here and if he has gone as I trust to his redeemer he has made a happy exchange." According to W. L. Webb in his *Centennial History of Independence,* Judge Easton, "a scholarly and brilliant man became incapacitated, and it fell to his sons-in-law, George Sibley and Archibald Gamble, to wind up his affairs." Despite the suffering Rufus Easton had experienced, through poor health, financial hardships, and political disappointments, he could not have been unhappy with the unwavering support of his first daughter. Mary saw her father every day and made his causes her own. When he died, he was put to rest at Linden Wood in a family plot laid out by George Sibley that still exists. Even though Mary expressed little of her sorrow in her journal, her father's death must have left a deep and irreplaceable void in her life. His passing closed a chapter in her life.

Mary did not have much time to grieve. She was not only busy with her school, but she had committed herself to a growing number of causes. One was the building of a proper Presbyterian church in St. Charles. Inertia continued to plague the building committee, and on May 12, 1835, more than two years after the elders had voted for the new building, Mary took the planning of the proposed church in hand. She told the elders exactly what they needed to do: "I believe it is the duty of the Session of the Church to visit *every member* of the Presbyterian Church of St. Charles to converse with them and take down their names either for the Church or against it." She instructed Mr. Black, Mr. Watson, and Mr. Campbell "to go in a body." She specified, "Not one of the three should stay behind—visit every member no matter where they are." She even told the three elders how they should word the petition they were to draw up and what to do with those church members who would not sign it: "Those who will not agree . . . let the Session after mildly admonishing them and requesting them to return to the church take down their names as concerned in promoting disorder and confusion and let them be summoned before the Session to answer for their conduct." In spite of Mary's efforts, the new building would not be completed until 1844.

Mary often insisted that her job at Linden Wood took up every waking hour. However, besides teaching at the Sabbath school and the African school and trying to run the Presbyterian church, she was also active in the Female Benevolent Society, helping those who were sick and/or impoverished. Through the Benevolent Society, she took up a variety of other causes, including starting a St. Charles chapter of the American Colonization Society, which had been founded in 1817 through the efforts of Presbyterian minister Robert Finley of New Jersey. In 1834, after hearing a speech by an agent of the Colonization Society, Mary decided "for the sake of example," even though she was already a member of the St. Louis auxiliary of the society, to start a new branch, as it was "a cause that I feel very much engaged in." The American Colonization Society provided what some saw as an alternative to emancipation. Its goal was to buy slaves and resettle them in west Africa along with free blacks. The society's greatest achievement was the formation of a colony that became the free country of Liberia. Finley's effort had gained the support of such prominent men as Francis Scott Key and Henry Clay, already a hero to the Easton/Sibley clan.

Mary's attitude toward slavery was ambivalent, as her father's had been. Although she wrote in her journal that slavery was "a stain on our national character," she and George had long owned slaves. Mary had taken Betty with her when she married, and George had a manservant who had served him since he first became a government agent. Three slaves were listed as part of the Sibleys' property when they borrowed money to build their home at Linden Wood. On their 1823 tax list, the Sibleys had claimed "five slaves, Abram, Betty, Henry, Edward, George, 3 boys," worth $1,500. Even though the Second Great Awakening embraced the ideals of emancipating slaves and abolishing slavery, the Sibleys owned slaves until 1859, when George emancipated his last remaining servant, Baltimore.

George and Mary Sibley found themselves in a dilemma faced by many intellectuals of their era, including Mary's brother-in-law Henry Geyer, who had married Mary's sister Joanna after the death of her first husband. Decades later, in 1856, Geyer would successfully argue against Dred and Harriet Scott's suit for freedom. Although Mary understood the evils of slavery and George realized that some slaveholders were evil, they favored a gradual approach to abolition. Mary's efforts to educate slave children reflected her belief in the power of education to make people independent. She felt that in teaching them to read and write she was preparing black children to achieve their own freedom. Whether or not Mary recognized it, the idea that education was power was revolutionary. George, on the other hand, thought that slavery would die a natural death, based on its economic limitations in an industrialized nation. He did not believe that slaves who were treated humanely suffered from their bondage, and therefore he did not support abolition.

The Sibleys, although ambivalent about the institution of slavery, could not have been immune to the growing movement for abolition. George debated his viewpoint with his friend Presbyterian minister Elijah Lovejoy, the editor of the *Alton Observer,* which became a decidedly abolitionist journal. When Lovejoy invited Sibley to write for the *Observer,* he declined. Moreover, George decided to cancel his subscription after Lovejoy published the Abolitionist Creed. As Sibley wrote Lovejoy on June 12, 1837, "so much in the *Observer* is seriously injurious to the cause of truth, religion, and sound philanthropy." He was opposed to having Lovejoy talk at the Presbyterian church on his visit to St. Charles on October 1, 1837, especially when he espoused the Abolitionist Creed. St. Charles slaveholders did not appreciate hearing that all men, regardless of their color, are equal or that slavery is "a legalized system of inconceivable injustice, and a sin against God." Later that day, a mob broke into Lovejoy's mother-in-law's house, where he was staying with his pregnant wife, and threatened his life. Not agreeing with him but realizing that Lovejoy's life was endangered, George Sibley and another friend, William Campbell, gave Lovejoy a horse, enabling him to escape St. Charles and return to Alton. Only five weeks later, a vigilante group killed Lovejoy in Alton, as he tried to defend his printing press.

Sibley was shocked by Lovejoy's murder, and it may have been at this time that he began divesting himself of slaves. Although both Sibleys supported the Back to Africa movement and the gradual emancipation of slaves, they had different ideas about racial equality. George Sibley never thought of blacks as equal to whites. When he emancipated Baltimore, who was forty-seven years old at the time, George wrote: "I do hereby emancipate, set free, and forever release said Baltimore, from all claims whatsoever. . . . He is honest and well

Abolitionist Elijah Parish Lovejoy was threatened by pro-slavery supporters when he spoke at the Presbyterian Church in St. Charles, but George Sibley and others managed to get him safely out of town. Lovejoy was killed by a mob in Alton, Illinois, in November 1837. (Dictionary of American Portraits, Illinois State Historical Society, courtesy State Historical Society of Missouri, Columbia)

disposed and capable of supporting himself reputably and usefully and I trust will continue to do so—If I were not well convinced of this he should not 'go out free' with my consent; firmly believing as I do and ever have, that with rare exceptions, the best position for the Negro race, in these states, for their own good, is that of . . . subordination to the White race." Mary, on the other hand, thought slave children were as capable of learning as were white children. She did not discriminate among the Native American, immigrant, slave, or female children she taught. She believed each child needed to be educated to be able to be independent, rather than "an object of charity" or "the object of scorn and rebuke." She pursued the ideal of education as the great equalizer, a progressive idea not shared by many at the time.

Despite the number of causes in which she involved herself, education and the cultivation of students at Linden Wood were of paramount importance to Mary Sibley during the 1830s. Her school grew to the point that she could not handle all the teaching and preside as headmistress. In 1836 Julia Strong, the wife of a Presbyterian minister, joined the faculty. The following year, Miss Eunice D. Rosseter became an "instructress" and joined the Presbyterian church. In an 1839 circular advertising Linden Wood, George Sibley wrote: "Miss

As Linden Wood Female College expanded, the Sibleys added on to their house to accommodate the growing number of boarding students. (State Historical Society of Missouri, Columbia)

Rosseter has had the benefit of *experience,* in some of the best and most celebrated eastern schools, and is, in all respects, well qualified for the station she has undertaken to fill." Sibley also proclaimed, "Well qualified assistants will be employed when necessary; and as it is intended that *the School at Linden Wood* shall be a permanent one, it is contemplated to make it contribute, in some degree, to elevate the character of our Western Literary Institutions." Pupils enrolled for a ten-month term, or a minimum of five months. They were encouraged to start the session that began the first Monday in September, or wait until the first week in February, and continue until the end of June. For the 1839 school year, one account claimed that close to thirty students enrolled, including the two daughters of Louisa and Archibald Gamble, who had been at Linden Wood since January 1, 1838.

George included in the 1839 advertisement a quotation from the *Richmond Compiler* that showed he did not abide by the widely disseminated belief in the inferiority of women:

Woman is the most important sex; and if but half of our race can be educated, let it be woman instead of man. Woman forms our character; *she* is with us through life; *she* nurses us in infancy; *she* watches us in sickness, soothes us in distress, and cheers us in the melancholy of old age. *Her* rank, determines that of her race: if she be high-minded and virtuous, with a soul thirsting for that which is lofty, true and disinterested, so it is with the race; if *she* be light and vain, with her heart set on trifles, fond only of pleasure, alas for the community where she is so—*it is ruined*!

Despite Linden Wood's position as a frontier school in a frontier town, the school was, philosophically, ahead of its eastern counterparts. The early nineteenth century saw many changes in education in the United States. Schools moved away from being primarily religious institutions, although many, like Linden Wood, maintained religious education and often had a connection to a church or denomination. Teachers explored new methods, including the Lancastrian model and the education through discovery promoted by Jean-Jacques Rousseau in France. Schools for infants were introduced in 1815. Elementary schools expanded beyond the three Rs, and high schools began giving instruction to students in different subject areas. English grammar became more formalized, and history began to be taught. In 1831 Samuel Goodrich published the *First Book of History,* designed for children nine to sixteen years old. School curricula of the 1830s incorporated science, fine arts, and physical education. Also during this era, the so-called National Period, women began to receive formal education beyond fancy needlework, drawing, and music.

Emma Willard, according to historians, was the first American woman to publicly support higher education for women. Mary Sibley knew about Mrs. Willard's seminary, which opened in Troy, New York, in 1821, and recorded in her journal that "it is encouraging to see what one female may affect by perseverance and diligence." She applauded Mrs. Willard's methods of teaching that did not involve the giving of prizes or rewards, which Mary thought to be a "pernicious system." Yet Mary noted, "There is yet much to be done toward maturing a good plan of female education. Whatever [women's] capacities may be, certainly that kind of knowledge called 'book knowledge' cannot be so necessary to them as to the other sex." Mary opposed any curriculum that would make "learned women at the expense of destroying their fitness for the peculiar duties allotted them in the station of life in which by the providence of God they have been designed to move." Although Mary believed women capable of learning science, math, and any other subject, she thought women should defer to the "nobler sex," who should be "looked up to as superior in knowledge" and strength. Linden Wood's program would thus include instruction in "Intellectual, Moral, and Domestic courses—based on the settled principles of *Christianity* and adapted to those on which are founded the free institutions of our own highly favoured country."

The curriculum at Linden Wood, from the outset, involved instruction in all branches of English—literature, grammar, writing, spelling, and elocution. For an additional fee, the school also offered instruction in French, music and piano, landscape painting, flower painting, and needlework—all considered womanly arts. Landscape painting was by far the most expensive course at ten dollars per month, considering that the English curriculum plus bedding, board, lights, books, and other supplies cost a girl's parents three dollars per week. Mary also believed that physical education was necessary, and she promoted Linden Wood as an environment that offered seclusion from noise and dust as well as ample grounds for recreation. When Mr. Nichols, the Presbyterian minister who had replaced Mr. Hall, spoke to Mary about the rumor that her girls were dancing by the piano, Mary countered that physical education was part of her program and "that during the weather in the winter when the girls could not get out to take exercise I had suffered them to dance by themselves to the Piano about . . . half of an hour in the evening after they had done their lessons for exercise." She informed "Mr. N." that she saw a great difference between dancing for exercise, a practice she could not imagine would be objectionable to God, and going to balls, something Mary tended to forget she had enjoyed when she was the age of her students.

Although Mary herself was not domestic and much preferred to allow a servant or a student take care of the necessities of cooking and cleaning, she did think it was important for women to learn domestic arts. Therefore, she provided instruction in cooking, cleaning, and sewing. She knew good cooking, and she liked to eat. One evening, after study and prayer, in thinking ahead to breakfast, Mary told her girls, "I want you to raise some buckwheat cakes for me tonight." According to the story told by Mary's niece, the next morning buckwheat dough was running under the kitchen door, as the girls had put a whole can of yeast into the cakes. Mary needed to leave domestic instruction to someone other than herself.

By the end of the 1830s, the school at Linden Wood had both a definite curriculum and an established routine. Mary as directress maintained strict discipline and bore responsibility for the curriculum as well as all aspects of student life. The girls' day began with an early class, followed by breakfast and morning prayers, then more classes, dinner, study, and supper. Bells announced the ending of classes and the beginning of meals. On Friday evenings the young ladies attended and participated in the St. Charles Singing School. On Sundays, attendance at church occupied the entire morning. During the afternoons Mary would often read the newspaper to the girls, encouraging them to locate on the map cities and other geographical features mentioned in the paper. Teaching "the habits of industry and care," Mary also required the girls to keep their sleeping and study rooms in good order. Basically, Mary regulated all of the young ladies' waking hours, both their recreation and their studies. She derived great pleasure in reading to them, entertaining them on her famous piano with the fife-and-drum attachment, and sitting around the fire embroidering with them. The 1839 circular stated: "As all the pupils admitted, must necessarily be boarders at Linden Wood, they will consequently be, at all times, under the care and observation of their Preceptresses. Their health, apparel, expenses, recreations, amusements, associations, manners and behaviour, will all be regarded with parental watchfulness."

Rules also governed the clothing of the Linden Wood girls. In the winter they wore black silk or worsted dresses with green cloaks; in the summer, white dresses with pink sashes. Bonnets were trimmed to match, with green ribbons in the winter and pink in the summer. Linden Wood required parents to provide their daughters with substantial walking shoes and whatever everyday clothing they might think proper. In an era of uniformly drab dress, Mary's love of bright colors was manifested in the ribbons she encouraged her pupils to wear. She, who in her younger days had piled her abundant hair on top of her head, now often wore a quaint lace cap over her curls, but it was always adorned with a ribbon—green, blue, pink, purple, or yellow, depending on the season and Mary's mood.

Mary Sibley also touched the girls' lives outside school. She wrote letters to her students when school was not in session and offered unsolicited advice about many subjects including courting, religion, and attire, as well as studies. In one letter to a "friend," a former student named Adie, Mary suggested that the reason Adie had not responded to an invitation to return to Linden Wood was because "your head is now filled with visiting, dress, and beaux." Mary admitted, "I do not say that such predispositions on the part of young ladies are wrong, for visiting is altogether proper and a duty at right times and at proper places, and as to dress a young lady should always think enough of dress to appear neat and genteel—and as to the beaux also, I have no objection provided they are such in character and standing as our parents and best friends approve." Then Mary spent two pages advising about the inquiries and observations necessary to secure the attention of the appropriate kind of man. She ended: "I have written much more than I intended on this subject, but all girls of your age are in danger of making an unwise choice and you will forgive me for being so prosy for the sake of the love I have for you and my desire for your usefulness as a Christian and happiness as an individual." To say that Mary touched the lives of her students would be an understatement.

Although Mary often wrote in her journal about her propensity toward indolence and procrastination, the journal itself seemed to be her only neglected pursuit. Her entries for 1833 and 1834 were sparse, and by 1835 she had obviously lost interest. Considering the number of causes she espoused, it is remarkable that she had time to write at all.

CHAPTER 9

Uncertain Times for Linden Wood

The second decade of the "Boarding School for Young Ladies at Linden Wood, Mo." did not begin or end auspiciously. In fact, the 1839 enrollment of thirty students proved to be the peak until Linden Wood became a Presbyterian college almost two decades later in 1857. Throughout the 1840s, the student population fluctuated between ten and twenty girls, and funds to keep the school open became a constant worry for Mary.

While trying to maintain Linden Wood, Mary did not let any of her other causes flag. Through the St. Charles Female Benevolent Society, she continued to teach at the African Sabbath school and at the Sunday school for immigrant children. She tended the sick and cared for orphans and widows. In her journal Mary described the day she brought an orphan child into Linden Wood to see if the Female Benevolent Society might consider giving the girl a scholarship to stay at the school since Mary could not afford to provide a scholarship herself. She also attended meetings of the American Colonization Society and joined the Temperance League. Thereafter she preached about the evils of drink to anyone who would listen. "Heard that Doc ———— drank hard," Mary wrote in her journal. "O' will the Lord have mercy upon him. There is nothing will save a man who has acquired this habit and make him fit either for this world or the world to come."

On January 24, 1840, Mary Sibley turned forty. She did not let her age bother her, nor she did lose any of her zest for various causes, but she did make a minor change in her lifestyle. At Fort Osage and later in St. Charles she had ridden horseback to visit friends and family and to carry out her duties for the Female Benevolent Society. Now

With the strong support of Mary Sibley, the Old Blue Presbyterian Church was finally completed in 1844. (St. Charles County Historical Society)

she decided it would be more fitting to ride in a carriage. The approach of her vehicle, which her students nicknamed the "Ship of Zion," inspired fear and awe. Since she was very fond of driving, Mary "made almost daily trips to town, to get the mail, if for no other business," according to Linden Wood's historian, Lucinda Templin. "She drove a white horse, very gentle . . . with a little negro perched up behind, to open gates." Mary's carriage also had a comfortable seat in the back in case she picked up a chance passenger to whom she could preach or from whom she could solicit funds. The distinctive appearance of the Ship of Zion announced Mary's arrival, welcome or not.

Seeing the Ship of Zion arrive definitely put the fear of God into the Presbyterian minister and the church elders, who despite Mary's insistence had still not built the new church. Mary had lost faith in them but continued to harp about the delay. "Procrastination is the thief of time," she preached to the preachers. Some years before, Mary had requested that a lot she owned in Alton be sold and the proceeds given to the church building fund. She had assumed that the lot was worth about $300, the amount she had pledged to the church fund in her journal if nowhere else. Now she learned that the value of the property might be as much as $1,400, so she vowed to sell half of the lot and "the other half if still unsold at my death, I wish my husband to appropriate to the same object, the building of the Presbyterian Church in St. Charles." Eventually, Mary would get her way. The Old Blue Presbyterian Church of St. Charles was completed in 1844, with the Sibleys contributing $859.57 toward the building and its furnishings.

Another person who was probably not always happy to see the Ship of Zion pull up to her door was Mary's mother. In her customary fashion, Mary offered her mother advice even when it was not wanted. After the death of Rufus Easton in 1834, Abial did become more dependent on her oldest daughter, and Mary told her mother how to handle her younger siblings. She advised her about their education and health issues and was always concerned about their salvation. When scattered cases of cholera occurred during the summer after her father's death, Mary feared that her youngest brother had symptoms of the disease. She did not believe her family deserved any special treatment, but she hoped that God would not let any harm befall Henry Clay Easton. When he survived Mary credited her prayers and supplications, but she could not convince her mother that religion had anything to do with Henry Clay's recovery.

After eight years of proselytizing from her daughter, Abial Easton remained adamantly against religion. "I have been much distressed to see my mother still obdurate and enraged against the cause of Christianity," Mary wrote in her journal. Her mother's lack of piety, she felt, was leading Abial to make poor decisions regarding Mary's youngest siblings. Abial was actually encouraging Alby, Sarah, and Medora "to go to public Balls—where their thoughts will be fixed on vain and sinful pursuits." Mary had apparently succeeded in forgetting her own youth and the balls she had attended, and she had become very protective of her younger sisters.

In 1836, when Alby was eighteen and still unmarried, Mary worried about the company she was keeping. She "went into town and intended to have a conversation with my mother, but did not have the resolution to do so." Instead, Mary sent her mother a note: "I cannot help letting you know the cause of my apprehension that you may guard her against the danger without her being aware of it. I believe

Joriah Brady is trying to court Alby and that she is inclined to encourage him. If her affections become engaged she will throw herself away on a dissipated fellow without character, without principle, and without any standing in respectable society." Mary advised her mother to take Alby and her youngest sisters, Sarah and Medora, and move to St. Louis where they could meet young men who were not "the dregs of society." Although Mary claimed she did not wish ill to come to Joriah or any other young men in St. Charles, she certainly could not bear the idea of her sisters "marrying such persons." Abial may have taken note of Mary's protestations, or it may have been coincidence that Alby met and, in 1840, married a St. Louis man, James S. Watson, who won Mary's approval. Neither of Mary's other sisters ended up marrying the "dregs of society." Sarah wed Col. Samuel South in 1842, and Medora married Abner Bartlett of New York in 1844.

The year Mary turned forty and Alby wed James Watson, their sister Russella died of consumption at age thirty-one. Life was fragile in the nineteenth century. George Sibley recorded news of deaths from cholera, yellow fever, "brain fever," miscarriages, stabbings, suicides, and unknown causes in his journal. He wrote about Mary's vigil for her niece, Mary Quarles Tunstall, who died despite Mary's care, leaving a husband and young children, "the eldest abt. 7 years old." Sibley also recorded the "burial of little Ludy" at Linden Wood. Louisa Gamble Easton, the first child of Henry Clay and Mary Blair Easton, was only fourteen months old when she died of "some brain affection." Sibley also wrote of the tragic fate of the Alderson family of St. Charles. Benjamin Amos Alderson lost his wife in March 1847 and buried his daughter Eunice beside her mother and infant sister on March 23, 1848. Four days later, George Alderson, aged four and a half, died of scarlet fever, followed on April 4 by Martha, "the eldest, abt. 8 yrs. old . . . buried . . . by the side of her sisters and brother, quietly and silently—very few people being present." Then on Sunday, April 9, 1848, "Mr. Alderson's third daughter Mary (abt. 6 yrs. old) died . . . and was interred at L.W. just after sunset. . . . Thus has Mr. Alderson been bereaved of Five of his Children with in 6 months."

Besides disease, a nationwide depression in 1842 had its effect in St. Charles. The Sibleys' school closed in 1843 because of financial problems and lack of enrollment. Not willing to give up her dream, Mary decided to travel to the East to solicit funds among her father's former colleagues, her friends from boarding school, and George

Sibley's connections. Convincing, beautiful, and accustomed to getting what she wanted, forty-three-year-old Mary returned to St. Charles with an endowment fund of $4,000, enough to reopen the school for the fall 1844 session.

Linden Wood girls began the 1844–1845 school year with renewed spirit. They delighted in creating a school song, "Clear the Way, Aunt Mary's Coming." Recognizing Mary's indomitable spirit, her students poked fun at the manner she had of always getting what she wanted. Mary not only allowed the girls to sing this song, a parody to the tune of "Dan Tucker," but she encouraged the girls to print copies for sale. "Clear the Way, Aunt Mary's Coming" sold for five cents a copy, providing another source of income for the struggling school.

In addition, the Linden Wood girls started a newspaper, *The Experiment.* Primarily concerned with fashion and design, the paper also featured political treatises, fiction, poetry, and stories on local personalities. The students frequently included information about the Sibleys. In one article they described Aunt Mary's homecoming after a recent trip. In another they wrote: "Uncle George has lately become quite a traveler, having visited St. Louis three times in as many weeks." Indeed, George's government jobs and his political interests took him away from Linden Wood often during the 1840s.

George Sibley had never lost his interest in politics. He ran for Congress as a Whig candidate in 1840 on the William Henry Harrison ticket. Harrison won, but Sibley lost. In 1844, George attended the Whig convention in Hannibal, Missouri, as a delegate from St. Charles. Later that spring, he traveled to the National Convention in Baltimore for the purpose of nominating Henry Clay for president. George, along with Mary's father, had long admired Clay, especially his American System, the plan that provided federal monies for roads, canals, and other improvements for states. However, George's aspirations for a federal office, as well as his hopes for Clay, were not to be fulfilled. Back in Missouri, he became a candidate for the state senate in 1844. He experienced another defeat, losing the election by forty-nine votes.

Mary always enjoyed discussing political matters. She supported her husband in his bids for election and campaigned for Henry Clay in his run for the presidency, writing letters to newspapers on Clay's behalf. She also worried about Clay's soul. On July 9, 1847, Mary was "led irresistibly to record" her feelings in her long-neglected journal:

"Reading in a newspaper 'Henry Clay' caught my eye and I read with emotion that on the 22nd June 'the Hon. Henry Clay was baptized in one of the beautiful ponds on his estate' . . . I have now evidence among many that our God is a hearer and answerer of prayers. For years I have prayed for the conversion of Henry Clay at times with fervency and faith—especially when he was run last for the presidency." Relieved about Clay, Mary Sibley could now take on the salvation of all those other people she feared might not be saved except by her, which included her students, her teachers, and her family.

Mary had always been concerned about her brother Alton, chiding him for not working hard enough in school and worrying when he dropped out of West Point and then out of medical school. Alton had gone on to become a colonel of the St. Louis Grays, had fought in the Black Hawk War in 1831–1832, and had been made commander of a battalion of five companies of volunteer infantry enlisted to fight in the Mexican War. On June 3, 1847, George Sibley proudly recorded, "Alton R. Easton left L.W. this morning for St. Louis whence he is to start in a few days for New Mexico . . . unanimously chosen Lt. Col. Commt. of this handsome battalion without any solicitation on his part." Before he left Linden Wood, Alton pledged his loyalty to a certain young lady, Elizabeth Ott, who was a teacher at the college and, like all other Linden Wood teachers, was a member of the Presbyterian church, having joined in 1845.

While Miss Ott waited for Alton to return from the Mexican War, another Linden Wood teacher, Eunice D. Rosseter, and the Reverend Samuel B. Smith of the Old Blue Presbyterian Church "were united in marriage at L.W.," according to George Sibley's 1847 journal. Alton married Elizabeth Ott in 1848, and the next year another family marriage took place when Mary's niece, Eliza Gamble, married John M. Clarkson in St. Louis. Mary attended this wedding, going upriver with her friend Mary Blair aboard the *Flyaway*, which she claimed to be a "most comfortable boat."

In the late 1840s, besides raising money and trying to reorganize Linden Wood as well as manage her various charitable activities, Mary had to cope with the shock of her mother's death. Alby Abial Smith Easton died on February 21, 1849, apparently without ever having become a Presbyterian. Mary, however, felt sure she had said enough prayers for her mother to save her. Abial was buried next to her husband in the small plot at Linden Wood.

Mary was also concerned about her husband's health. He had always been frail, and he pushed himself, taking on demanding duties that required travel and caused stress. After his unsuccessful bid for the state senate in 1844, he had apparently given up hope for a political office, but in 1849 Sibley served as a delegate to the National Railroad Convention in St. Louis. Then in 1851, at the age of sixty-nine, he accepted an appointment to the Board of Managers to direct and organize a state asylum at Fulton. In his seventieth year, Sibley assumed the responsibility of working with a delegation in St. Charles to devise an improvement initiative for the town, "some feasible plan to commence a system of Artificial Roads in the County." After 1851, George became a semi-invalid and spent most of his time at home working on improvement projects for St. Charles as well as taking on the almost full-time role of establishing Linden Wood as a college for women.

After her mother's death, Mary continued to mother her younger siblings, even though they were now all adults. Even the baby of the family, Henry Clay Easton, was twenty-three years old and married, therefore not easily influenced by his indomitable sister. However, in 1851, at age fifty-one, Mary at last had the chance to become a real mother through the untimely death of her sister-in-law Elizabeth Lloyd Beall Easton.

Mary's brother Langdon, fourteen years her junior, was serving in the U.S. Army. His first daughter, Medora Abial Easton, was born on October 26, 1848, at Fort Leavenworth in Indian Country. When his wife gave birth to their second daughter on July 15, 1850, Langdon was garrisoned in Santa Fe. An illness, possibly yellow fever, took the life of the young, weakened mother just five days later. According to George Sibley's journal, the wife of a soldier of the Garrison of Santa Fe, a Mrs. Drysdal, "having lost her own infant just about the time of Mrs. Easton's death, took the infant Bettie to nurse and had her in charge 'till their arrival at L.Wood." On Monday, September 8, 1851, George wrote that, after a journey of thirty-three days, "Capt. Langdon C. Easton of the U.S. Army arrived here today from New Mexico via Ft. Leavenworth—he brought with him the Remains of his Wife who died in Sta. Fe in July 1850 leaving three children, one a few days old, another abt. a year old, & the other a boy abt. 8 yrs. old by her former marriage with Lt. Porter son of Com. David Porter," who had been killed in the Mexican War.

On the afternoon of Langdon's arrival, his wife was interred in the family burial ground at Linden Wood. Of the three children, the older two are not mentioned again in George Sibley's diary or in accounts of visitors to the Sibley household. Elizabeth's eight-year-old son was presumably taken to live with his Porter relatives in Mexico, Missouri, where Elizabeth's first husband had owned a farm. Medora Abial Easton may have remained in the care of the Sibleys for a brief time or have been taken to her grandmother Mary Beall. The youngest was taken in by George and Mary Sibley. On Sunday, March 28, 1852, according to George's journal, the Sibleys participated in communion at the Presbyterian church and had "the little daughter of Capt. Langdon C. Easton, now 20 months old, now in charge of Mrs. Sibley," baptized Elizabeth Lloyd Easton, after her mother. Bettie, as they called Elizabeth, became Mary's youngest student.

Meanwhile, Mary and George Sibley continued to try to resolve the financial issues that had plagued Linden Wood throughout the 1840s. Even though the school had reopened in 1844 after a year's hiatus, by 1850 the Sibleys had determined that to make Linden Wood a full-fledged college they would need to seek an endowment and incorporation by the Presbyterian Church. In 1852 George Sibley wrote his friend Samuel S. Watson, suggesting he "as a member of the Synod to select a college site consider Linden Wood as a possible location." Mary also expressed her desire to transfer the school to the Presbyterians and stated that "for my part I prefer the means should come from our own people and the management of the institution should be in the hands of Presbyterians. There cannot be much harmony without it. I would not have anything to do with a school from which religion was excluded and it is important that it should be the right kind of religion." Mary was referring to differences that had arisen between the New School Presbyterians, who associated with the abolitionists, and the Old School Presbyterians, who leaned toward free will and the right to own slaves. Presbyterian minister Samuel J. P. Anderson also supported the Sibleys' cause: "I believe no one thing so exactly meets our wants as that which you propose. The daughters of the church have been far too much overlooked in our schemes of education and we all know the commanding influence of the mothers. We will go to work at once to prepare and present to the legislature a suitable charter." Anderson proved to be an effective spokesman, and one month later Linden Wood was granted a charter.

On February 24, 1853, Linden Wood Female College became incorporated as one of only seventeen permanent Presbyterian institutions of higher learning established in the South before the Civil War. George and Mary Sibley donated 120 acres of land to the college in a quitclaim deed along with their orchards, fields, and buildings. Judge and Mrs. Samuel Watson, who had helped secure the support of the Presbyterian Synod and were probably the Sibleys' closest friends, agreed to give the school another 160 acres plus $1,000 if the Presbyterian Church could raise $20,000 within six months from January 1, 1853. These funds provided the means to erect the first school building. Later, the Watsons, who had no children, donated $5,000 unconditionally for the construction and $4,000 for the furnishings of the building. By the end of 1853, Mary Sibley felt she and her husband had accomplished their long mission. Mary Sibley wrote Reverend Anderson remarking on the travails of establishing a permanent school for women:

> Our school had to struggle through much opposition, abuse, and slander due to the fact that it was strictly a Presbyterian school at the time when such schools were not the fashion and when Protestants were so much afraid of being considered sectarian they would not sustain our own schools. I consider our school the first that lifted up the standard of opposition to convent education in the West.

Linden Wood was now a full-fledged women's college instead of the combination grammar and finishing school for girls that Mary Sibley had run. The Presbytery appointed a fifteen-man board of directors, which included Archibald Gamble, to hire teachers, to develop the curriculum, and to manage the school. The Sibleys would assume a new role, one that was more parental than administrative. However, these changes took four years to complete, and the Presbytery did not actually began running the school until 1857.

Following the 1853 incorporation of the college, Mary continued to be at the school every day, and she assumed her fund-raising role once more in 1854, when the school again closed because of financial difficulties. A general economic slump affected the whole nation as the country edged toward war. Desperately wanting to make the new college building a reality, Mary went on another tour of the East to secure funding. It was perhaps at this time that she met Susan B. Anthony and began espousing female suffrage, although no documents have been located to verify the friendship that Lucinda Templin reported existed between the two women. Mary Sibley and Susan Anthony did have similar ideas. Mary had always believed that women held influence in American society, and the right to vote would be a natural extension of the rights of *educated* women. Again, Mary's power of persuasion and her positive attitude prevailed in her fund-raising campaign. She collected $8,000 among her friends and those of her husband, more than half of that needed for construction of the new hall. The Presbyterian church and local individuals, including the Sibleys' friends Judge and Mrs. Samuel Watson, supplied the remainder of the funds needed.

Meanwhile, the Presbyterians renewed their efforts to endow the college and to make Linden Wood the equal of any institute of higher learning in the country. The Presbytery appointed Reverend S. M. Sneed as the agent to solicit funds and, at the same time, issued a nineteen-point statement about the college. The publication included the fact that the Sibley estate was valued at $30,000 and that Major Sibley had stated in making his quitclaim deed: "The bequest is made upon full reflection, and *is intended to be irrevocable.*" Although the college would be under the control of the Presbyterian church, it would at the same time be "*free from sectarianism* and based on such large and evangelical views that all who love the Bible may share its benefits." The Presbytery maintained that Linden Wood would be a primary, collegiate, and normal school for young ladies to provide thorough instruction and also help them acquire the art of teaching. The board hoped that many of the teachers of Missouri would be trained and educated at Linden Wood, though it also hoped the school would serve not only Missouri but the entire Mississippi Valley.

The Presbytery intended the college to "enlighten, ennoble, and elevate our daughters, that it might secure the approbation and patronage of the public; not a frivolous boarding school, which would unfit its pupils for the trials and duties of life, but one in which solid attainments, should be acquired, and one in which young women should be prepared to occupy with eminent honors the sphere in which they may be placed." This last statement came very close to the one written by Mary Sibley more than twenty years earlier when she insisted that young girls receive an education in which

Sibley Hall has changed somewhat over the years but remains a monument to Mary and George Sibley, who dedicated their lives to promoting education. (Wolferman photo)

"essential knowledge," including domestic chores, was combined with a "liberal education."

Both of the Sibleys continued to play leading roles in the establishment of the new Linden Wood. In 1856, George personally took on the job of building supervisor when the building committee "let the matter drop." First, he sanctioned a fifteen-hundred-square-yard plot to be used as a "burying place." It already included the tombs of Rufus and Abial Easton, Elizabeth Lloyd Beall Easton, and several members of the Presbyterian Church. Then he drew up the plans for the school, described by former student Delia Gibbs as a brick "square box of a building, with a pepperbox of a cupola on top," a fair description of the old Sibley Hall. When the building was remodeled in 1926, a colonnaded front porch and wings on each side softened the original architecture. Sibley recorded all the transactions for the new building in his journal, including the sum of $13,800 that Bigelow and Son estimated the building would cost.

Excavation began on June 3, 1856, and the cornerstone was laid during the Fourth of July celebration. Ever the keeper of Linden

Wood history, George took special pains to determine the items that would be placed into the cornerstone. In a tin box that was seven inches square, he packed twenty-five documents that he thought would be "of future interest to the history of Linden Wood," including copies of the Act of Incorporation and George and Mary Sibley's quitclaim deed to their land, a paper giving a history of the college, a Bible, an annual report of the Missouri State Colonization Society, and a copy of the *Missouri Gazette,* the first newspaper published west of the Mississippi. These documents were "well secured from damp by thick canvas glued on, then covered with five coats of water proof paint." Sibley noted in his journal: "The box thus prepared was then placed in the cavity of the corner stone (the Southeast corner) under the hammered range stone fronting Eastward—completely bedded in and covered with plaster-of-Paris." The cornerstone was cemented into place in mid-July, and the building took a little more than a year to complete.

Sibley paid attention to every detail of construction. He chose the bricks, the floor coverings, the wood. He decided on the "mortise lock" front doors and inside doors with white knobs. Insisting on the best materials, George made sure the windows were premium quality, glazed Pittsburg Glass. He demanded that all the woodwork have "two coats of the best American white lead and boiled oil" and be "finished with a third coat of such colours as may be selected and approved." By July 1857, Linden Wood had a permanent building that looked worthy of a real college. It stood three stories high, above the basement. Modern conveniences included furnaces and rosin gas lighting.

The new building housed the kitchen, dining room, library, and dormitories. The first floor, according to Delia, who was a student from 1856 to 1864, held "reception offices, the President's study, emerging rooms, and living quarters for President Schenck, his wife, son Willie, and Grandpa Carey (Mrs. Schenck's father)." Lest anyone think Grandpa Carey was just there because he needed housing, Delia added that "this dear old man of eighty" grew all the vegetables and fruit, drove old Dobbin into town twice a day for mail regardless of the weather, played the melodeon at evening services, and wrote poetry. Of the Reverend Addison Van Court Schenck, Delia remarked only that he was "a man of pleasing address, and I think generally liked." Delia also remembered Willie quite well and wrote that he had died of typhoid fever while at the college. He was buried in the graveyard in back of the new building beneath a tombstone marked only "Willie."

Above the offices and the Schencks' residence, the second and third floors had dormitory rooms on both sides of the hall. A teacher lived on each floor at the end of the back hall. The rooms, again according to Delia, "were light, clean, and comfortable, but very plain. The furniture consisted of a wooden bed, comfortable mattress, clean but narrow covers, so scant that sometimes a fist fight was hardly avoided; dresser, stand, two straight wooden chairs, and a strip of carpet before the bed." While all the "housekeeping" (Delia's term) took place in the new brick building, girls continued to use the old frame building for classes.

The wooden structure that had served as the Sibleys' home since they had moved to Linden Wood "had been built as necessity required," according to Delia, as she reminisced during the 1927 centennial celebration of Linden Wood. "There were many narrow stairways and passages, and odd-shaped rooms, and porches made into rooms, the floors of which always seemed to me to be at an angle of about sixty degrees. There were pianos in these porch rooms and the girls practiced there. Altogether, it was a weird sort of a structure, which did not take the girls long to declare was haunted." Until the Sibleys moved to a new house off campus, they lived in the east part of the frame structure and poked fun at the girls for their fear of going into certain parts of the building alone. George and Mary Sibley, however, agreed with their students that there were plenty of strange noises and that the school was indeed haunted, if only by rodents.

As the construction of the Linden Wood building began, the Sibleys began construction of a two-story brick house just west of the college grounds. They had land enough for a small farm, and Mary planted her characteristic red geraniums. She also dressed herself and her niece Bettie in the bright-colored clothing she loved. Mrs. Charles Gauss, a former Linden Wood student and a childhood playmate of Bettie's, whose mother, Jane A. Durfee, had "attended Mrs. Sibley's first school," told of an overnight visit at the Sibleys' home. On Sunday morning, Mrs. Sibley brought out new merino or cashmere cloaks she had had made for herself and for Bettie. Her own cape was bright blue, and Bettie's was red. Bettie hated her new cloak so much that she "shed tears," according to Mrs. Gauss, "but had to wear it nevertheless."

Mary continued to be at the school every day until the Presbyterians took over, but George was now mostly bedridden. He read copiously and wrote on current topics for several papers. The couple received many guests in their new home. They had a large dining room, which held George's white-linen-draped bed at one end. When Presbyterian elders or others came for dinner, they would eat and talk at the dining table, and George could join in the conversation while he drank soup or gruel through a silver straw. He was considered a great intellectual and a fine entertainer, and guests were happy to receive invitations to dine with the Sibleys.

Mrs. Charles Gauss remembered Mary as a good housekeeper and cook. "She did not do it herself . . . but knew how to make others do it. I remember how appetizing her meals were, her batter-cakes especially something not easily forgotten." Mrs. Gauss also recalled how wonderful the grounds of the Sibley house were but regretted when "Bettie and I were called in from play to spend some time in sewing or reading, or to listen to Mrs. Sibley as she gave us religious instruction. It was intended for our good, but I am afraid the time seemed to us 'tedious and tasteless,' with a pony to ride, and a sure-enough, vine-covered playhouse in the yard. . . . We had a little cooking stove and it is a wonder we didn't burn ourselves to death." Mrs. Gauss also remembered Aunt Mary playing the piano; "one of her pieces, descriptive of a battle was a great favorite," especially since "much to our delight" Mary made ample use of the fife-and-drum attachment. Mary obviously continued to play multiple roles as mother, teacher, and religious instructor.

CHAPTER 10

A Real College

On September 6, 1857, Linden Wood College opened as a Presbyterian school with eighty students and "an adequate corps of teachers," according to the board of governors' report. Delia Gibbs, who has given us such a detailed image of what the school was like in 1857, was a day student. In fact, half of the students must have been day students, since only forty boarders could be accommodated, unlike the old days when all Linden Wood girls were boarders. Delia described the typical school day as beginning with chapel exercises: a reading of the Scriptures, the singing of a hymn, a short talk by the president, and a prayer before the girls repaired to Bible study classes. Every teacher had a Bible class, and the Bible was considered one of the school's textbooks. The day began at 8:00 a.m. when the days were long and at 9:00 a.m. when the days were short. Seven-hour school days were the norm.

Judging by the curriculum, a seven-hour school day must have meant seven hours of classes. The freshman courses included elocution, orthography, ancient history, Latin (Caesar), geography, Greek, natural science, and Bible study. The senior curriculum included elocution, Shakespeare, astronomy, history of civilizations, Latin (Cicero), Greek (Homer), geology, intellectual philosophy, French literature, German (Schiller, Goethe), and the Bible. Obviously, the niceties of embroidery and dance were not the mainstays of the curriculum. Although Linden Wood had never been just a finishing school, the new college raised the level of academic demands. The students were the daughters of gentry, however, and they were always expected to act like ladies. Apparently, those expectations carried forward. A 1936 freshman at Lindenwood College recalled that at convocation the dean "emphasized that we were there to study, not to learn how to balance a teacup on our knees; we were supposed to know that already."

The new Linden Wood, according to the 1863 catalog, divided the school into four courses of study: preparatory, collegiate, normal, and fine arts. The preparatory school was geared toward training young women for the freshman year in college. It offered a thorough survey of all branches of ordinary English education, but it also served as a complete school in itself for those young ladies who would not go on to college. The collegiate course of study, according to the school catalog, "could not ordinarily be completed in less than four years." When students finished the college curriculum, they received a degree of either mistress of English literature for those who satisfactorily completed the English course with one language, or mistress of arts for those who completed the scientific, literary, and classical course. The aim of the school was "to prepare young ladies for the responsible positions they will fill in after life—to fit them for usefulness here, and happiness hereafter."

The first commencement ceremonies after the new building had opened were held on June 12, 1858. The *St. Charles Reveille* reported that the events reflected the "character of Linden Wood, with its large and beautiful edifice, and ample ground, amid the calm and sylvan beauty of surrounding nature; and based on the immovable foundation of the Protestant faith." The principles of Mary Sibley's school had not changed since she had founded it. The financial underpinnings were finally in place to keep the school going.

With Reverend Schenck at the helm of Linden Wood, Mary did not need to be in attendance every day. She could spend time with her invalid husband, tend her gardens, meet with her various committees, take care of her house, fulfill her charity work, and mind Bettie. As the years had passed, Mary's intensity had not lessened. In fact, she probably became more eccentric with age, and she certainly continued to get whatever she wanted. For example, in 1860, when Mary was about to turn sixty, she determined that she would like to have her birthday dinner with her friends Mr. and Mrs. W. P. Gibbs, Delia's parents. Before going for dinner, she informed the Gibbses' cook to "tell your mistress" that she was coming, "and I want you to be sure to have broiled chicken and beaten biscuits." Of course, her wishes were granted, and she appeared for dinner in an odd costume of a satin-striped low-cut dress with her long bright-blue cape.

Meanwhile, George Sibley stayed home. Despite his infirmity, he continued to read voluminously and write. He also monitored Linden Wood's accounts to verify that the trust that he and Mary had deeded to the school was being honored. In 1860, he discovered that the members of the board of directors were selling off college endowment land in order to pay debts on buildings and cover incidental expenses. He expressed his outrage to the current president of the college, John Jay Johns: "Already has too much of that property been frittered away to serve purposes quite foreign to the object originally intended. . . . The land was not endowed to building or to pay off debts but to form an endowment fund—purpose—to charge as low a tuition as possible." Despite Sibley's written objections, the board of the directors continued to sell off property in lieu of any other alternative to paying college debts.

The year of Mary's sixtieth birthday brought Civil War fears closer to reality. By the following spring of 1861, the war had come to Missouri. Encounters between state militia and federal troops resulted in continuing bloodshed. On May 10, after federal troops captured Camp Jackson, a state militia encampment on the outskirts of St. Louis, a crowd gathered as the captives were marched away, taunting and throwing stones at the inexperienced federal troops. Someone began firing into the crowd, and twenty-eight civilians, including women and children, died. Efforts by state and federal representatives to reach agreement failed, and in June state officials fled as federal troops occupied Jefferson City. Federal forces defeated the state militia at the battle of Boonville, and on July 31 a provisional Unionist government was installed in Jefferson City. One of the bloodiest battles of the war was fought at Wilson's Creek, twelve miles southwest of Springfield, Missouri, on August 10. Gov. Claiborne Fox Jackson and other deposed state officials determined to create a government-in-exile in Texas and join the Confederates. Although Missouri remained in the Union under the provisional government, led by Hamilton Gamble, the brother of Archibald Gamble, it also had a star on the Confederate flag. The divided loyalty of its citizens led to fierce guerrilla warfare during the war years and beyond.

In this time of war, Linden Wood also suffered. Parents were afraid to send their daughters away from home. According to Mary's niece Mary Sibley Easton Kloes (the daughter of her brother Joseph):

Those in charge of the college were equally anxious about keeping them. However, Mrs. Sibley was undaunted by conditions around her. She painted a large flag and had it placed over the college as an emblem of peace. "The Linden Wood emblem" became famous. It was eight feet long, and six feet wide, and inside the circle was a second circle of red stars, thirty-four in number; in the center the word "Love" was painted in large blue letters. Two olive branches crossed beneath the word, completing the design.

Mary Sibley was going to forge ahead through the turmoil and keep a positive attitude.

Mary's strength was sorely tested on January 31, 1863, when the love of her life, George Sibley, died at age eighty-one. He had been an invalid for many years but had remained so involved and productive that Mary seemed shocked that he had succumbed. He died in the house he and Mary had built ten years earlier and was buried in the graveyard he had laid out at Linden Wood. On his tombstone, as he had requested, was engraved Psalm 96, verse seven: "Return unto thy rest, O my soul, for the Lord hath dealt bountifully with thee."

After George's death, Mary tried to continue as though nothing had happened. She refused to wear the customary black and carried on without showing her mourning, saying she did not want to upset the girls. Her friends, however, knew that her outward demeanor hid a very deep hurt. Evidence of her grief was her decision to sell the house she and George had built, even though her friends the Watsons had built a house next door and she was surrounded by other friends and supporters. Without heeding anyone's advice, she sold her home quickly to Capt. John Shaw and moved in 1864 to a house she built near Lafayette Park in St. Louis. She was close to her niece Virginia Gamble Gibson and to her sister Louisa Gamble.

In St. Louis, she resumed the eccentric behavior for which she had been known in St. Charles. One day she visited one of her nieces—Alby's daughter, Mrs. John Donaldson—and saw a handsome spread on the bed. "Well, I like that. I'll just take it," Mary said, and take it she did. After the spread was confiscated, Mary's relatives made it their business to hide any special thing they did not want to lose when Aunt Mary was due to visit. Nonetheless, they all liked to please her and joked about her ways.

Mary also traveled some after her husband died. In the previous two decades, she had gone on fund-raising trips to the East and to

St. Louis Mo.

By the mid-nineteenth century St. Louis was much different from the frontier city in which Mary Sibley had grown up. (Eduard Robyn lithograph, State Historical Society of Missouri, Columbia)

visit her sister who lived in New York. She had frequently visited family members in Palmyra and St. Louis. Now she went back often to visit the Watsons and the Gibbses in St. Charles. Reportedly, she also took several trips to Europe and on at least one occasion went to Milwaukee, where she met a man who asked her to marry him. Louise Gibson Conn, Mary's great-niece who lived in St. Louis, recalled that Mary, who was "a very pretty old lady," appeared one day in Lafayette Park arm-in-arm with her beau, who was "hobbling along with a cane. In those days we had concerts in Lafayette Park in the afternoon," Louise explained. "They were attended by the nice people and it was quite a meeting place for the belles and beaux." After the sighting, Aunt Mary reportedly asked her niece privately, "What would you do with a beau?" to which Louise replied that, personally, she would put him on six months' probation. Aunt Mary replied, "I'll just do that." The beau died before the six months had passed.

Another incident remembered by Louise demonstrated Mary's lifelong love of teaching and of riding horses and driving carriages. Mary "was very fond of driving and when she came to town and visited at my mother's she liked to drive in the afternoon. Our carriage driver's name was Jake. He had formerly been a slave but had been freed, and he lived with us until his death. Aunt Mary used to drive out with Jake and she always insisted on sitting on the outside seat.

As she aged, Mary Sibley wore a lace cap over her
hair, but it was always decorated with colored ribbons. (State Historical Society of Missouri,
Columbia)

One of the friends she often visited was Mrs. Peugnet. She would say,
'Now, Jake, it is spelled P-e-u-g-n-e-t,' which of course, was all lost to
Jake," since he had never learned to read or write.

Although Mary had relatives in St. Louis, she was not entirely
happy away from her beloved Linden Wood. She also proved to be a
poor manager of money, another indication that she was lost without George. Delia Gibbs related that Mary was "very close in small
things, but liberal in great ones." She went on, "I think she was com-
pelled to sell her home in St. Louis." In any case, sometime in the mid
to late 1860s, Mary moved back to St. Charles and built a cottage near
the college. She was pleased to find that, in her absence, her girls had
not forgotten her or George.

Linden Wood drew Mary back to St. Charles, and she lived near her beloved campus for her remaining years. (State Historical Society of Missouri, Columbia)

The Sibley Society, a debate club, had been established in 1863 to honor George Sibley. The purpose of the society was to encourage literary attainment. According to Lucinda Templin, its constitution stated, "No person, male or female, [was] eligible for membership who was not *distinguished* for talent and versed in some science, or art." The club held weekly debates and rendered decisions on a variety of topics: "Is the hope of reward a greater incentive to exertion than the fear of punishment?" "Is the mind of women inferior to that of man?" "Which exerts the greater influence, the man of wealth, or the man of talent?" Through this debate club, women studied parliamentary law, practiced standing before an audience and presenting ideas in a clear and convincing way, and learned how to think. This role for women was a novel idea in the 1860s and one George Sibley would have heartily approved, as did Mary.

Back in St. Charles, Mary became very involved in a Protestant sisterhood. The House of Bethany was a nondenominational, evangelical organization of women "willing to devote one or more years of Christian labor as volunteers." Joining this group was indeed an indication of Mary's great faith, as the sisters of the House of Bethany were required to wear drab dark-gray uniforms, not at all Mary's style. In 1866 Mary became the secretary for the House of Bethany and began keeping a journal for the society. She had let her own spiritual journal lapse. Even though her last entry had been in 1858, she had recorded no more than ten pages during the preceding ten years. Now she took up record keeping with her usual style, as if she was on a personal mission from God. According to Mary's 1868 entries, the sisters made 2,000 visits to families and distributed 87,884 religious tracts. In May she wrote: "Found a woman on 2nd Street very sick lying upon the floor in very destitute circumstances—called in a physician for her, got her prescriptions filled and supported her present wants—left her in the care of the Lord—asking to be with her." In other entries she talked about placing orphaned children in mission schools, taking meals to families, distributing Protestant literature, giving lessons, and caring for the sick.

Mary also joined the Second Adventist Church in her late sixties. This Protestant sect, established by William Miller, a Baptist, believed that in 1843 or 1844 Jesus would have a second coming and would rule for a thousand years on earth. In 1845, when Christ had still not appeared, the Second Adventists, who after the Civil War became Seventh Day Adventists, predicted that Jesus' return would occur at some indefinite time in the future. Therefore, believers needed to live a pure life, abstaining from alcohol, tea, coffee, and tobacco. Adventists believed that prayer, charitable work, and participation in a missionary program would ensure them the opportunity to be "translated," or born again, when the time came. Mary perhaps took comfort in the idea that she would return to earth and could carry on with her good deeds.

Mary's faith led her to decide that she had at least one more important role to play during her current lifetime. She resolved to become a missionary to Japan. Although her friends advised her that she was both too feeble and too hard of hearing to undertake a trip to Japan, she was determined. At the age of seventy-one, Mary went to New York, sailed to Panama, and then traveled to San Francisco, whence she planned to take a boat to Japan. However, her rough ocean voyage convinced her, when her friends and family could not, that she did not want to undertake the arduous sea route to Japan. She viewed this thwarted trip as a failure, one of the few times in her life that she did not do what she set out to do.

No sooner had Mary returned from San Francisco than she took up the cause of trying to bring young Japanese women to the United States to be educated in a Christian environment. If she could not go to the mission, she would have the mission come to her. A series of letters with Isaac K. Yok Yama, a Japanese student at the Theological Seminary in Fairfax County, Virginia, indicate that Isaac had enlisted Mary's help to bring his sisters to Linden Wood. Dr. Hepburn, who was the head of the Presbyterian Missionary at Yokohama, Japan, where Mary had been going originally, thought Isaac and Mary's ideas were absurd. He said the United States was "no place for Japanese girls" as "they will be more apt to learn things that will be of no use to them about dress and fashion and the follies of our so-called civilization; they would be only unfitted for their Japanese homes, and people." Isaac disputed Dr. Hepburn's arguments. He wrote Mary, "It is [a] dreadful, awful, and horrible thing to be a heathen. Which do you rather prefer to learn the dress and fashion of civilization or heathen customs, such as idolatry, profaneness, sabbath-breaking, cutting eyebrow, dying teeth, slavery to husband (that is all women are treated like slaves by their own husbands) evil company, etc.?" Although Isaac admitted to not being knowledgeable about missionary work, he implored Mary: "Dear Madam will you be kind enough to think about all these causes and try to get my sisters in some way by the help of God?"

At the age of seventy-three, Mary apparently again raised money, this time to secure passage for two Japanese girls from Yokohama to San Francisco to Ogden, Utah, and then via the Central Pacific Railroad Company to St. Charles. Isaac had convinced Mary not only that his sisters needed a Christian education but also that after they received their education they could return to Japan with the necessary knowledge for missionary work. "I will write as soon as possible to my father and sisters about this glad tiding," Isaac wrote Mary, "and no doubt they will rejoice, and gladly will come to this enlightened Christian land, as soon as they can." Again, Mary had accomplished what she set out to do, if not in her usual fashion. When she

A new headstone marks Mary Sibley's grave, acknowledging her as the founder of Lindenwood. (Wolferman photo)

was not able to personally forge ahead, with others clearing the way, she cleared a path that enabled others to accomplish her goals.

Mary Sibley's late years were little different from her early ones. She maintained her vitality and physical strength and remained known for her vivaciousness, intelligence, and diligence about what she considered to be her duties.

On Thursday, June 20, 1878, at the age of seventy-eight, Mary Sibley died in her sleep. Many of her friends, family, and students came to her funeral, held at the Jefferson Street Presbyterian Church, which she had helped build. According to a St. Louis paper: "A number of St. Louis citizens went to St. Charles on the morning train, and most of the citizens of St. Charles attended the funeral. She was as well and widely known as any lady in the State." Forty-five years earlier, Mary had written in her journal, "We often seek the applause of the world in what we do. May this never be my governing motive in anything." Although Mary did not seek public recognition, those who attended her funeral paid their respects and applauded what she had accomplished.

Mary Sibley was buried at Linden Wood in the plot that her husband had laid out, resting beside her father, Rufus Easton; her mother, Alby Abial Smith Easton; her sister-in-law, Elizabeth Beall Easton; her husband, George Sibley; and little Willie, the son of the first president of Linden Wood.

CHAPTER 11

Mary's Legacy

Mary Sibley did not dwell on the fact that she was mortal. In fact, her great-niece Louise Gibson Conn claimed that Aunt Mary never thought she would die. Because she had become an ardent Second Adventist, Mary assumed she would be "translated," which fit in perfectly with her lifelong philosophy, which was to always think about the here and now and not worry about the future. Mary did not plan far ahead, because she had so many short-term goals to accomplish. After Mary Sibley's death, her descendants realized she had not only left her mark wherever she had been, but she had planned her will so carefully that her estate was settled without dispute or disharmony.

Following Mary's death on June 20, 1878, her family gathered at her home in St. Charles. Her brother Col. Alton Rufus Easton came down from St. Louis on June 21 along with two of Mary's nieces, Russella Easton Watson Walker and Alby Watson Donaldson, both daughters of Mary's sister Alby. Mrs. Donaldson and Mrs. Walker "went out to Mrs. Mary E. Sibley's late residence," Alton wrote in the court record, "while I went to the bank; when I arrived at Mrs. M.E. Sibley's house, Mrs. Donaldson and Mrs. Walker told me they had not been able to find her will. They handed me a portfolio of papers and after examining them, I found an open envelope containing the foregoing instruments of writing purporting to be the last will and codicil of said Mary Easton Sibley, the testatrix, written on six pages of notepaper." The document, which Alton assured the court clerk was written in his sister's hand, had been signed and witnessed in September 1877 and then amended in February 1878 when Mary added a codicil. Perhaps the deaths of her sister Alby in February 1877 and her brother Joseph in March 1877 had made Mary realize that she should get her affairs in order.

Mary's will provided for more than thirty personal bequests. She returned to her nieces and nephews and great-nieces and great-nephews the very items she had "stolen" from their parents. She had apparently been mindful of what she was doing when she said, "Well, I like that; I'll just take it," as she whipped a bedspread off a niece's guest bed or commandeered a book that she wanted to "look over." Mary's will appears to be a disorganized list of repetitive names and gifts, given the extent to which family names recurred in each generation. However, Mary made sure that each of her surviving siblings received a bequest and that the survivors of the one brother and three sisters who had predeceased her were also remembered.

Mary left her first bequest to the relative with whom she had the closest ties, Elizabeth "Bettie" Lloyd Easton Morton, whom she had raised and who had also witnessed her will. For some reason Bettie's sister Medora Abial Easton Walker is not mentioned in the will. The answer could be as simple as the fact that Mary and George Sibley did not know Medora, who was raised elsewhere. Bettie, however, had remained close to her Aunt Mary and Uncle George, even after she left Linden Wood, married Maj. Charles Morton, and moved from Missouri. The Mortons' first child, Emmet Crawford Morton, was born in October 1877 at Fort Laramie. They then returned to Jefferson Barracks in Missouri, where they were when Mary died and where Sibley Morton was born in January 1880. Mary stipulated that Bettie's endowment—all of her jewelry, half of the family silver, all of her clothes, and her new parlor carpet as well as her Bible and prayer book, and fifteen hundred dollars—was "to be paid before any of the other bequests."

Mary then remembered her siblings. To her youngest sister, Medora Easton Bartlett of New York City, who had been born twenty-three years after Mary, she gave one thousand dollars and one-half of the family silver plate. She also stipulated that at Medora's death her inheritance would be divided between her two daughters, Grace and Mary, and that Medora's son would receive lots number 22 and 23 in the "Sibley Addition, City of St. Charles." Mary gave her brother Joseph's widow, Jane Charlotte Smith Easton, of Hannibal, Missouri, her lady's writing desk and a large easy chair. Mary also remembered that Joseph's fourth daughter, Sarah Easton, wanted her "patent kitchen safe." To her brother Langdon Chevis Easton, Mary bequeathed lot number 2 in the Sibley Addition, while her youngest brother, Henry Clay Easton, received her hanging bookshelves and bookcase. Mary's sister Sarah Easton South acquired all of Mary's pictures, two new quilts, and all the table linens, while Sarah's daughter Medora took possession of a large mattress, a bedroom carpet, and a stair carpet. Mary's sister Louisa Baker Easton Gamble, wife of Archibald and mother of eight Gambles, gained a set of green-and-white china and a table. Alby Abial Easton Plant, Mary's brother Alton's daughter by his first wife, Eliza Ott, received Mary's silk quilt along with two pieces of silver to pass on to her oldest daughter. Mary left Emma Noye Easton, her brother Alton's second wife, a china catchall along with a Marseilles quilt that had once belonged to Mary's mother. Russella Watson Walker and Alby Watson Donaldson, daughters of her deceased sister Alby Abial Easton Watson, were also remembered. Keeping track of her six sisters and four brothers and their offspring, many of whom had nearly identical names, must have been a difficult task for Mary as well as for the executors of the will.

Besides the many personal gifts Mary Sibley left, she also endowed her two favorite institutions: Linden Wood College and the Presbyterian Church of the United States. To Linden Wood, she gave lot number 7 as well as all the ground known as the "Sibley Addition to the City of St. Charles," with the provision that the land should be rented until twenty thousand dollars had accumulated. These monies, to be called the "Mary Sibley Fund," would then be used to provide loans for young women interested in pursuing an education at Linden Wood to become Christian teachers. To the Presbyterian Church, Mary gave one lot on Clay Street as well as any funds left after the rest of her bequests had been made. The leftover money would be called the "George Sibley Fund" and used to assist young men who wanted to prepare for the ministry. After appointing her youngest brother, Henry Clay Easton, trustee along with Henry A. Cunningham, Mary signed and dated her handwritten will on September 8, 1877, nine months before her death.

In February, Mary added a codicil to provide for "a young, friendless girl named Rosanna McGuire" whom Mary had taken under her care. Mary wished her executors to provide this young lady with "a sufficient sum to clothe her and pay for her education at Linden Wood College." Mary's life had been dedicated to giving young women and young men the opportunity for an education, and her last word was that Rosanna McGuire deserved that chance.

The old stone gates of Lindenwood, the "King's Gate," are located on old Kingshighway and welcome students to today's coeducational university. (Wolferman photo)

Mary's greatest legacy is the college she founded. Today Lindenwood University, internationally known for its innovation and dedication to students, offers more than one hundred undergraduate and graduate degrees. The school's mission statement is little different from Mary Sibley's original: "We believe that education is the way to personal freedom and responsibility, which are the keystones of any democracy." Mary preached this philosophy to Indian children, African Americans in her Sabbath school, immigrant students, and Linden Wood girls. Her goal of educating each student to "become a self-sufficient, effective, contributing citizen" is continuing.

Lindenwood often struggled financially after Mary's death, especially during poor economic times. In the late 1980s, the school nearly closed. In 1989, when Dennis C. Spellman became the twentieth president, the school's enrollment was down to fewer than eight hundred students. The school's endowment was less than one million dollars, and the campus had shrunk to eighty acres. The board and President Spellman dedicated themselves to taking Lindenwood "back to its roots," emphasizing the goals of Mary Sibley's initial mission statement. During the seventeen years of Spellman's presidency, the school saw substantial enrollment growth and the construction of nine new buildings. Spellman explained the college's success as going back to "The Lindenwood Way," which emphasized teaching a cohesive curriculum of general knowledge. As students, faculty, and alumni mourned the death of Spellman in 2006 they also celebrated the growth in enrollment. Lindenwood had nearly 15,000 men and women enrolled during the 2007–2008 school year.

The five-hundred-acre campus in St. Charles retains much of its original charm. The entrance to the college begins at the historic stone Linden Wood gate, and the street into the campus is still lined with linden trees. Sibley Hall, the oldest and for some years the only building, stands regally at the end of the tree-lined drive and now serves as a women's dormitory. The new buildings blend in with the original one, and the beautiful trees make for a bucolic setting. The burial plot laid out so long ago by George Sibley remains behind Sibley Hall.

In June 2005, Lindenwood was ranked as Missouri's "fastest growing four-year college or university." The rebirth of Lindenwood was based, according to Spellman, on the mission of the university's founder, Mary Easton Sibley. Certainly, Lindenwood and the graduates of the university, both the men and the women, are Mary Sibley's greatest legacy. She cleared the way for women to become more independent and for all children to have the right to an education, regardless of their race, wealth, or background. Mary Sibley left her mark, not just at Linden Wood but everywhere she went. "Aunt Mary's Coming" was not only a warning but a salute!

For Further Reading

Almost all of my research on Mary Easton Sibley involved primary documents, especially diaries and letters. Mary Sibley's journal was of great importance in providing insight into her life and thought. Secondary sources included newspaper and journal articles as well as two works by college dean and historian Lucinda de Leftwich Templin, *Reminiscences of Lindenwood College: A Souvenir for the Homecoming* and "Two Illustrious Pioneers in the Education of Women in Missouri: An Address," both written in 1926 for Lindenwood's bicentennial. Both are of limited availability and were written before Mary Sibley's journal came to light.

Valuable books on early St. Louis and its French founding families include *The First Chouteaus: River Barons of Early St. Louis,* by William Foley and C. David Rice (Urbana: University of Illinois Press, 1983); *Before Lewis and Clark: The Story of the Chouteaus, the French Dynasty That Ruled America's Frontiers,* by Shirley Chisholm (New York: Farrar, Straus, and Giroux, 2004); *Duels and the Roots of Violence in Missouri,* by Dick Steward (Columbia: University of Missouri Press, 2000), and two books by William Foley: *The Genesis of Missouri: From Wilderness Outpost to Statehood* (Columbia: University of Missouri Press, 1989) and *Wilderness Journey: The Life of William Clark* (Columbia: University of Missouri Press, 2004).

Books on education and educators of the nineteenth century include *The Peabody Sisters: Three Women Who Ignited American Romanticism,* by Megan Marshall (New York: Houghton Mifflin, 2005). Alma Lutz has written about influential nineteenth-century women, including *Emma Willard: Pioneer Educator of American Women* (Boston: Beacon, 1964). Catherine Clinton's work includes

The Other Civil War: American Women in the Nineteenth Century, rev. ed. (New York: Hill and Wang, 1999). In order to better understand how women were viewed in America, I found sections of Alexis de Tocqueville's *Democracy in America* enlightening; Martha Sexton's *Being Good: Women's Moral Values in Early America* (New York: Hill and Wang, 2003) includes a section about St. Louis.

George Sibley's journals proved helpful and very interesting. His early journals from Fort Osage, *Seeking a Newer World: The Fort Osage Journals and Letters of George Sibley, 1808–1811,* edited by Jeffrey E. Smith (St. Charles: Lindenwood University Press, 2003), explain what the fort was like before Mary Sibley arrived on the scene. Of special note is the publication edited by Kate L. Gregg: *The Road to Santa Fe: The Journal and Diaries of George Champlin Sibley* (Santa Fe: University of New Mexico Press, 1952).

For the Osage Indians and the time Mary and George Sibley lived at Fort Osage, I relied on the research I did for *The Osage in Missouri* (Columbia: University of Missouri Press, 1997) and on the classic *The Osages: Children of the Middle Waters* by John Joseph Mathews (Norman: University of Oklahoma Press, 1961).

Many other books mention Mary Sibley but lack detail. James Michener's *Centennial* (New York: Random House, 1974) catches her spirit. She certainly would have been thrilled to see herself as Michener described her.

Index

advice to sisters, 119–20; concerning
Henry Clay's soul, 121–22
Sprague, Otis, 68, 69–70
St. Ange de Belrive, Capt. Louis (French
lieutenant general of Louisiana), 20
St. Charles Female Benevolent Society.
See Female Benevolent Society
St. Charles: as subdistrict of District of
Louisiana, 17; district court, 20;
Western Engineer passes through, 60;
as temporary capital of Missouri, 64,
66; Eastons make home in, 83; Santa
Fe commissioners meet in, 87; Sibleys
move to, 87, 89; history of, 88–89;
cholera epidemics in, 100, 108, 119
Stearnes, Catherine, 71
Ste. Genevieve: Rufus Easton attends
meeting in, 2–3, 15,
Stevens, Joseph, 58
Steward, Dick, 33
St. Louis Fur Trading Co., 32, 40
St. Louis Grays, 122
St. Louis: as capital of District of
Louisiana, 2; establishment of, 3–4;
in 1804, 3; as fur trading center, 6–7;
under Spanish rule, 7; attacked during Revolutionary War, 7–8; under
French rule, 9, 11; hosts Lewis and
Clark, 8–9; ceremony to transfer
Louisiana Territory to U.S., 9–10,
illustration of, 10; territorial convention of 1804, 13; in 1804, 15–17; as
capital of Territory of Louisiana, 20;
post office of, 21–22; in 1809, 33;
schools in, 34, 36; during New
Madrid earthquake, 41; during War
of 1812, 41, 42–43; social life in
1816, 52–53; *Western Engineer* passes
through, 60; Santa Fe commissioners
meet in, 83; Mary moves to Lafayette
Park, 134
St. Martin, Pierre, 36
Stoddard, Captain Amos: as acting governor of Upper Louisiana, 9, 11;
relationship with French clique, 9,
11, 12–13, 17; as acting civil commander of District of Louisiana, 12;
leads Indian delegation as departing

governor, 22
Storrs, Augustus, 80
Strong, Catherine, 71
Strong, Julia, 111
Subfactory of Fort Osage, 62, 66–67, 74
Subscription schools, 56
Suffrage, 126
Sunday school. *See* Sabbath school

Taos, New Mexico, 85–86
Temperance League, 117
Templin, Lucinda de Leftwich, 43, 94,
118, 126, 137
Territory of Louisiana, 17, 20
Territory of Orleans, 12, 13
Tevis, Julia Ann Hieronymus, 43–44
Tilliers, Rudolph: factor at Fort
Bellefontaine, 24; dismisses Sibley,
29, 30
Tompkins, George, 36
Tracy and Wahrendorff, 90, 92
Trading business, 4–5, 6, 7, 30
Trading house law, 50, 74; closes trading
houses, 79
Trading posts: at Fort Chartres, 3; in St.
Louis, 3–4, 15; during War of 1812,
42; new posts opened after War of
1812, 59. *See also* Factories
Treaty of Fort Clark (Osage) of 1808,
30–31, 40, 42, 43
Treaty of Ghent, 42
Treaty of Paris, 3
Treaty of Portage des Sioux, 43
Treaty of St. Louis (Sac and Fox) of
1804, 19, 27, 43
Treaty with Kansa Indians, 58–59;
about Santa Fe Trail, 84–85
Treaty with Osage: of 1818, 59; of 1822,
75; of 1825, 82; at Council Grove,
84;
Truteau, Jean Baptiste, 34
Tunstall, Mary Quarles, 120

Union Mission, 67
United Foreign Missionary Society of
New York, 67
Upper Louisiana, 2, 9, 23, 24, 88. *See
also* District of Louisiana

ABOUT THE AUTHOR

Kristie C. Wolferman is author of *The Osage in Missouri* and *The Nelson-Atkins Museum of Art: Culture Comes to Kansas City*, both published by the University of Missouri Press. She lives in Kansas City, Missouri, and Pinehurst, North Carolina.